Tough Turf is tough talk. Bill Sanders wants to spend some time with you because he cares about you. Are you happy with the person you see in the mirror? He'll help you become your own best friend. You'll find a number of strategies for becoming more popular, taking a stand for your beliefs, improving your grades, getting along better with your parents and kid sister—just take a look and find the area where you think you need help the most.

You're a special person who deserves the best that life has to offer. You're encouraged to dream—and follow the road to making those dreams come true. Bill Sanders shows you how to steer clear of such roadblocks as a poor self-image, shirking responsibilities, and negative peer pressure. He also shares real-life stories about kids like you which prove that traveling the hazardous routes of drinking, drug abuse, and premarital sex can lead to dead ends. *Tough Turf* will point you in the direction of success and happiness and encourage you to stay there.

Bill Sanders

A TEEN SURVIVAL
MANUAL

Power Books

Fleming H. Revell Company
Old Tappan, New Jersey

Scripture quotations in this volume are based on the King James Version of the Bible.

Library of Congress Cataloging-in-Publication Data

Sanders, Bill, 1951–
    Tough turf.

    Bibliography: p.
    Summary: Advice for teenagers on how to come to terms
with themselves and how to deal with the stresses and
pressures of the world around them. Also discusses the
effects of drugs and alcohol and how to deal with
addiction.
    1. Youth—United States. 2. Adolescent psychology—
United States. 3. Self-respect. 4. Youth—United States
—Drug use. [1. Conduct of life. 2. Drug abuse.
3. Alcoholism] I. Title.
HQ796.S247   1986   305.2′35′0973   85-30023
ISBN 0-8007-5212-0

TO my wife, Holly, who has always believed in me. When things got tough, she believed some more.

TO my mother and father, who taught me what true commitment in raising a family was all about.

TO Emily, who daily shows me laughter, love, and that God is still in the miracle business.

TO my mother-in-law, who never thought I'd get out of my sealer clothes.

CONTENTS

BEFORE YOU START

Welcome aboard to a book I hope you'll find one of the most important ones you ever read. Your English teacher may never recommend it as great literature (and how many of you would read it, if he did?); it won't give you a clue as to the cure for cancer; but it can do something very personal—help you make the most of your life. I've aimed at challenging you, giving you a hand, and making you feel good about yourself and the things you can accomplish with your life.

No matter who you are, what you look like, or how many friends you have, this book is meant for you: today's teenager. Right now you face some of the hardest years in your life. The tough-turf years never seemed easy to anyone, but today's teens probably have the roughest time in our country's history, when it comes to being a young person moving into adulthood. You confront many pressure situations—and the stakes are for real! The world plays for keeps and doesn't care who or what it rolls over in the process.

As I've put this together I've tried to be honest with you. I don't beat around the bush. I've been a teen, I've talked with teens, I've worked with teens, and I know how you feel, what you think about, what your cares are, and something of the world you live in. That's why I wrote this book. In you I see a part of my future. Because you are a part of my country's future, when I invest in you, I invest in myself, my family, and my country's tomorrow.

I designed this book as an action plan you can look over, choose what fits you, and follow the step-by-step formulas it outlines. You won't have to read page after page or an entire chapter to find strategies on how to become more popular, tips on how to overcome peer pressure, or ways to raise your self-esteem. They'll shout at you from every page. I've also tried to make it fast moving, enjoyable, motivating, encouraging, and practical.

How to Read This Book

Before you begin serious reading, you'll probably want to take a quick trip through the book, looking at titles and the how-to lists it contains. If you find an area where you need help right now, go to that section and read it first, then go back and read the book from start to finish. The first section, which deals with your self-esteem really forms the basis for the rest, because no matter what your trouble—handling peer pressure, drugs, popularity, or maybe getting good grades—how you deal with it will depend on your opinion of yourself. Once we've made you your own best friend, we can answer all the other questions you'll want to ask.

Keep a highlighting pencil or pen in hand as you go through this book. Mark it up. Underline what really grabs you. Maybe you'll want to tear out pages and put them in your room for instant reminders. In short, whatever you do, *get involved* with this book. It can only help you if you give it your best shot.

Next, share what you learn with friends and family members. If you like some of the book's suggestions and plan on using them, share them with those close to you. Challenge them to better themselves right along with you. Make this world a better place, and do it with a friend, study group, or a family member. Of course, you'll find that the best way to make the world a better world is to start by making you a better you. That's what we're going to do right now.

Part 1
MY TURF

-1-

LOOK AT ME, WORLD, I'M SOMEBODY SPECIAL!

Everyone has some ideas about who's special in the world. What's yours? Maybe you could write a list of sports heroes and heroines, movie stars, or other people who seem to stand out in a crowd. *These* people seem really important!

I felt that way not long ago, during one of the most exciting experiences of my life. Was this me, *Bill Sanders*, on the camera crew with NFL Films during a "Monday Night Football" game? I could hardly believe I had an opportunity to get an up-front view of the Detroit Lions playing against the L.A. Raiders. Yet my friend John Gross had invited me to be his helper and film carrier during the game, which meant I could go everywhere with him: on the field before and during the game; in the locker room and press room, for interviews with the players, after the game; and in the ABC announcing room, talking with superstars such as

13

O. J. Simpson, Dandy Don Meredith, and Frank Gifford.
WOW!

As we arrived at the Pontiac Silverdome three hours before
kickoff, my heart rapidly pounded, and I anticipated a fun-
filled, action-packed evening. It was exactly what I expected
and even more. I learned several things that will have an impact on my life for many years to come.

Who's Important?

When John said, "Go over and look inside that room.
That's where O. J. and the guys will do the live broadcast," I
began my first lesson. As I stood at the door, staring at the
headphones and equipment and watching the ABC attendants
getting everything ready, my mind raced back seventeen years,
when I was sixteen years old. I felt as though I were in high
school as I stood there. I kept saying to myself, *I can't be here.
This is just a dream. I'm not good enough to be around all
these superstars. They're all famous and rich, and I'm a nobody. Just a skinny kid from a little town, whom no one knows
or cares about. No one back at school will believe that I'm actually here. I'll need proof.*

Just then I heard several people say, "We've got to get an
interview with O. J. His rushing record was broken yesterday."

I slid back to my dream. *That's it. I'll shake O. J.'s hand.
Maybe then they'll believe me. Or maybe a picture—but I
wouldn't have the nerve to ask him for a picture. What if he
asks me for my name and school? I'd be so nervous I'd probably forget. How like me to forget my own name.*

A tug on my jacket interrupted my thoughts. Next to me
stood a scruffy-faced older man in worn-out clothes, with his
two crutches beside him, trying to get my attention. I thought,
*Don't bother me, you nothing! I'm looking in the ABC an-
nouncers' booth. You probably don't even know who will be
sitting here in less than an hour.* Then, *What if someone sees
me talking to this guy? And how did he get in here, anyway?*
That man sure didn't *look* special. Why should I bother with
him?

But as my mind snapped back to the present I heard him tell me: "I'm supposed to be in there at halftime, telling them about my miracle marathon and how I did it." Realizing there was more here than met the eye, I whipped out my small tape recorder, held it up to him, and got this amazing true story.

His name, he said was Captain Jim Leather, though most folks just called him Captain Jim. When I spoke to him he'd just finished a 3,129-mile marathon from Raleigh, North Carolina, to San Diego—on one leg! The entire trip took 214 days, but Captain Jim could never have accomplished it alone. Because it was God and him together who made it, he called it a miracle marathon.

Before the marathon, Captain Jim had been told he would never walk again. Confined to a wheelchair, there seemed little hope for him. But this determined man prayed and trained and prayed and trained. At the end of his feat, even news reporters who didn't believe in God told him, "Man, you've made a believer out of me!"

Nine years earlier, he told me, Joe Gibbs of the Washington Redskins had turned him on to Jesus. The football star shared his faith with a man who had lost a leg to cancer at the age of ten—a seeming nobody. Captain Jim told me that he had no reason to get out of that chair before Joe Gibbs spoke to him, but through their conversation, the football star had helped change the life of one of his fans.

Because I work with teens, speaking to them all across America, I asked what advice he would give to young people who don't believe in themselves. Without hesitation and with belief in his eye, he told me to tell them to get a dream, a goal! First you need to pray to God that it is right, then *go for it!* Find some people who have accomplished your dream, write them, and discover where you want to be. You can get much help from such people. Then you'll have to put your all into achieving it—your energy, your time, your training. But when you achieve it, you'll be somebody. If he could do it at fifty, he said, an American teenager could certainly reach his dream, with all that was going for him.

As I shook Captain Jim's hand and said good-bye I realized

what an opportunity I'd almost missed. While gazing into that announcer's room, dreaming of stardom, I failed to see the beauty at my very fingertips. I felt ashamed to think that I didn't want to be seen with him. In ten minutes I learned more about being a winner at life and turning dreams into reality than I have ever learned watching a three-hour football game.

All of a sudden one person's definition of a football game seemed to make a lot of sense. He described it as a time when 60,000 people who need exercise pay good money to sit in the stands and watch twenty-two on the field, who don't!

The game hadn't even started when I saw O. J. in action. Not on the field or behind the cameras. He was waiting to give an interview, with game time only thirty minutes away. After a long day he had a lot to do to get ready for kickoff. Instead, he showed real professionalism. He displayed respect for others, not getting mad at the newspeople as they waited for the right moment to do a live interview. Patiently and politely he chatted with us and let us take our pictures with him.

Someone asked him, "Are you upset that your rushing record was broken?"

"Absolutely not!" he replied, "I love to watch good runners. I love the game and the chance to watch other professionals. I never look back. I keep looking ahead at my career and what great things I can accomplish in the future." I felt impressed with the way O. J. treated others as if they were important, too.

As I walked out I bumped into Dandy Don Meredith, announcer for "Monday Night Football." I said, "Are you . . . ?"

"I was this morning," he told me. What would he tell teenagers thinking of dropping out of school? I asked.

The Lipton Tea twinkle sparkled in his eye as he replied, "Don't be a fool. Stay in school!"

"What about self-esteem? What do you tell young adults who don't believe in themselves?"

"Look at life realistically. We all *aren't* created equal. Each of us has different talents and abilities. Look at what you've got and make the most of it. There are abilities in each and everyone of us. My advice to the young person is, 'Find your strong points, work hard at them, and be proud of yourself.'"

As he walked away I stood in a new kind of awe. Not the awe I experienced an hour earlier, anticipating the presence of people whom I thought were better than me, but the awe of realizing that people can reach the top of their professions by dedication, prayer, hard work, being nice to others, and believing in themselves.

Just being the best at their jobs didn't make these men great. Their examples showed me it took more than that. They became *real* winners at life because, even though everyone else treated them as if they were important, they still had the humility to treat others as special people.

You don't have to play football professionally to be a star. You don't need to have the prettiest face in your class. Winners at life come in all sizes, shapes, and colors. How we feel about ourselves on the inside is more important than how we look on the outside.

When a Loser's a Winner

The game was exciting. I stayed right beside John everywhere he went: running up and down the sidelines, following the play—then to the end zone, less than ten yards from the players as the Lions made a beautiful goal-line stand. You'll know I'm a die-hard Lions' fan when I tell you they lost 24 to 3.

But I can't see that as a losing night. I watched winners in action. In the fourth quarter I stood by the Lions' bench. Many Lions' fans (the kind who only cheer when you win) began booing and really bad-mouthing Lions' coach Monti Clark. Gary Danielson, the quarterback for Detroit (who had been booed earlier), walked over to the fans and said, "Hey, give him a break. He works awful hard. He deserves more respect than that." What a winning attitude to stick by your coach, no matter what!

After the game ended, I followed the press people into the interview room. They had cameras and fancy taping equipment, which they used for their interviews. Right then I remembered my little pocket tape recorder. No one knew me. I told myself, *Get going, you'll never have another opportunity like this again.*

Gary Danielson was walking out, as he had finished his interviews with the newspapers and TV stations. I walked over to him and introduced myself. I thought, *I'm not from the press. He won't talk to me.* Boy, was I wrong. For ten minutes he shared his life with me. He told me how he doesn't equate this loss or this losing season with his overall success in life. He said, "When I was a kid, I was good at sports. Many of the other kids didn't get picked when we were choosing teams. Today they are the doctors and lawyers and have successful businesses." He continued, "I was fortunate to have a family who loved me and believed in me. I know many young people don't have close families. They need to work hard at what they are good at. They can make it ... I know they can. If they really want to and try!" I thanked him for his time and words.

Then I saw one of the most respected players in the NFL: Lions' defensive player Doug English (I just thought those guys were big on TV. He was no baby!). I told him my name and shared how I travel across the country, talking to young people about self-esteem, goal setting, and how to build a successful future. In response he spoke about how he couldn't even make his high school football team as a starter until he reached his senior year, but some coaches believed in his abilities and encouraged him to keep practicing after everyone else had gone home. Hard work and believing in God and himself made him into a success. What influences in his childhood enabled him to believe in himself? I asked. He said, "Number one, my parents bragged on me. Number two, they loved each other, and number three, I was brought up in the church." He explained how his belief in God has gotten him through the rough times in his life. Though we met as strangers, we parted as friends.

As I drove home with John late that night, I shared all the wisdom-filled examples I have just shared with you. We both grew that day, never again to be the same.

So What Does It Mean to Me?

Maybe you're asking yourself why I'm telling you all these stories. After all, you're probably not a football player. Maybe you don't even want to go out for a team. How can it help you?

What I'm trying to show you is that success means something more than playing Big League ball. It's more than being well-known. No matter who you are, no matter what your life looks like right now, *you* are important. Only one of you exists in the entire universe. Like snowflakes, your fingerprints and voice are totally unique. If a famous Rembrandt painting costs $1 million because it's one of a kind, you are worth at least $1 billion.

I don't care if your friends haven't told you how much they need your friendship—or if you don't have any friends at all. Perhaps your family is a mess—they're too busy or broken up—and you haven't heard an "I love you" in so long you can't remember what it sounds like. No matter what life seems like right now, you are important, and we can make it through together. One day at a time—one moment at a time, if necessary. If Captain Jim made it 3,129 miles on one leg, on both you can walk toward your dreams. You only need good self-esteem.

What Can Good Self-esteem Do for a Teen?

I'm not talking about nice theories here. What I want to share with you really works. I've seen it change lives.

When I was eighteen years old I saw an ad for Big Brothers of America. It made me sad, because I kept thinking of the time my dad spent with me as I grew up, and I wanted to do something for at least one little guy. So I signed on to help someone.

When I first met Curt, the boy I worked with in Big Brothers, that eight-year-old kid felt too afraid to look me in the eye. But we worked together on Curt's self-esteem. More than fourteen years later, I'm proud of the self-assured, compassionate man he has become. At twenty-two, Curt owns his own business. Boosting his self-esteem helped make him achieve success today.

Since then I've gone on to have a career as a professional speaker. For the past five years I've spoken in high schools, and at state and national conventions, juvenile homes, prisons, teacher in-service sessions, and for many businesses. But wherever I meet and work with teens, I find that the basis of all their needs lies in the way they feel about themselves. I've tried to show them how to help themselves, and the ideas I give them are the same ones you'll find in this book. You, too, can have the kind of success story one girl had, after she heard me speak in a detention center.

I had just spoken to about 500 young people from all kinds of backgrounds—mostly bad. Afterwards I went to the back of the auditorium and shook every hand as they left. One girl waited behind, asked one of the officers if she could talk to me, and was granted ten minutes. She told me I saved her life during my speech. She explained, "My dad committed suicide when I was three years old. All my life I didn't have to look for trouble, it found me. Everytime I did something wrong, my mom and teachers would say, 'You're just like your dad.' I've heard it a million times, so I figured I might as well commit suicide, too. Three times I've tried it in the last year. The first time, I'll admit, I just wanted attention, but without the grace of God I wouldn't be here today after the other two. Today you kept telling me that God made me and that I'm special and unique. At first I didn't believe you, mostly because I didn't think you really cared. You made me laugh, and you kept telling me I had greatness in me. Something happened; I started believing you. Now I've got hope. It won't be easy, but these people here really care. I know I can make it now."

For years she had believed in the opinion everyone else seemed to have of her. But that's not the way to a clear picture of yourself. Maybe you aren't about to kill yourself, like that girl, but it's the same for you. You can't live on someone else's thoughts about who you are or how you should be. There is greatness in you, and we're going to work in the next chapter to help it come out.

Check Out Your Turf

1. Who do you think is special? Make a list of some of your heroes or heroines. Why are they important to you? Why do you admire them? List some of the elements that make them *real* winners.

2. List some people in your life who are real winners, even though they may not be superstars. What makes them winners? How can they help *you* become a winner through their examples?

3. When have you thought you were a loser? Why did you feel that way? What did you do about it?

4. When have you felt others were losers? Why did you feel that way? Did you do anything about it? How can you help others who are losers? What do you think of Reggie Smith's words: "We're not born winners, and we're not born losers. We're all born choosers!"?

-2-

MY SELF-ESTEEM (HOW GOOD IS IT?)

I won't tell you I had the greatest image of myself as a teen. As you'll see later, I couldn't give the jocks any competition, and I didn't win any prizes when it came to grades. Being tall and skinny didn't help, either. Everyone kidded me about it at school.

In the eleventh grade I got a chance to start all over. When my dad got a job in another town, I moved from a Class-D high school in a small town to a Class-A high school in my new hometown. I never knew they built schools so big. Maybe my old school had twenty doors in the whole place (including the rest rooms). Now I had to contend with two floors, six wings, homerooms, and 1 *million lockers!* (At least it *seemed* like 1 million lockers.)

You might not believe this, but it took me three weeks to find my locker. I caught the bus in the morning and went to school. With barely enough time to go to all my classes and catch the bus at night, how could I look for my locker? So I kept my books in with a friend's.

After I moved, I felt so shy that he was the only person I got to know.

Can you imagine that? I make a living talking about self-confidence and believing in yourself, but as a teen I couldn't even find my own locker. It probably doesn't take much to figure that something happened to change my opinion of myself. In this book I hope to give you some of the ideas I later came in touch with, so that you won't have to wait three weeks to find *your* locker, if you move.

Let's Take a Look at Self-esteem

Before we examine your self-esteem, let me point out several very important things.

1. No one has a perfect self-esteem. By this, I mean that no one feels totally happy with himself all the time. Everyone has ups and downs. Having bad days is perfectly normal. If I never had my low times, I wouldn't appreciate the good ones, and I wouldn't have anything to strive for.

2. Self-esteem (how you feel about yourself) responds to exercise like a muscle. It might seem shabby now, but with effort and practice, it can grow as strong as anyone's. That's right! No matter how low you feel about yourself today—you can apply certain principles and practice certain techniques to raise your self-esteem to a happy, healthy level. Start getting excited now about the positive you in the future!

3. We'll take inventory on how you see you. (The self-esteem-quotient quiz will come up soon.) Realize this. Everyone has negative parts in his self-esteem. Once you've identified yours, you can work on these areas if you choose. Notice, I said *if* you choose. It remains entirely up to you what you do about the actions and beliefs in your life that drag you down and keep you from feeling great about yourself. No one can or will do it for you. I must say I feel proud of you for sticking with this

book so far. You started on your way. Don't stop now!

In the following test place a check beside the sentence or situation that best fits you: For each number you'll check the column that describes your reaction most closely. You'll have some answers in each column if you're honest. We will grade it when you finish.

Test Your SEQ (Self-esteem Quotient)

Negative If you have a low self-esteem (you don't believe in yourself):	Positive If you have a high self-esteem (you believe in yourself):
1. I expect to fail most of the time.	1. I expect to be successful most of the time (grades, relationships, and so on).
2. I can't stand it if others laugh at me.	2. It doesn't bother me if people laugh. I figure it's their problem, not mine.
3. I don't have many friends, and I am very jealous!	3. I have lots of friends and I give my boyfriend or girlfriend the freedom he or she needs.
4. I feel uneasy when I am alone.	4. I enjoy being alone at times, because I am my best friend.
5. My attitude is, *It doesn't matter what I do. I don't care anyway.*	5. I have a good attitude toward people, my future, school, my family, church, and so on.
6. I hate criticism, and I get mad at the person who tries to help me.	6. I appreciate someone pointing out areas in which I can grow or become more effective.
7. I blame others.	7. I take responsibility for my actions, grades, and life.
8. It's almost impossible for me to forgive or forget that someone hurt or made fun of me.	8. I forgive others easily, because I know I make the same mistakes.
9. I feel successful when I have lots of new clothes, a giant record collection, a new car, computer, and so on. (I love my material things.)	9. Material items are not nearly as important to me as people. I never flaunt my material things, because I would not want to hurt those who are less fortunate.

10. I think, *No one wants to go on a date with me.*

11. I'm loud in class and during assemblies. I figure, *Why should others enjoy it and learn? I'm not going to.*
12. I go along with the crowd most of the time.

13. I join in with others when they are putting someone down.

14. I only do what is expected of me and no more on my job.

15. I come late to my job and take long breaks. Besides, everyone else does.
16. I accept a date with just about anyone.

17. I smoke cigarettes.

18. I go to any movie, especially if it is a top hit.

19. Sex before marriage is okay if you love someone.

20. I don't like my height, weight, ears, teeth, family, race, or color of skin.

10. I think, *She'll probably love to go out with me. I'll go ask her.* (If she says no, I say to myself, *You're not as smart as I thought you were!*)
11. My respect for other people allows me to be quiet when others are talking.
12. I like being with the right crowds, but I always decide for myself what is good enough for me to do.
13. I've developed the courage to stand up for the person getting picked on.
14. I'm not the world's greatest worker, but I do try my best. I also look for extra ways I can be a good employee.
15. I'm no worse than my word. If I say I will be there at 3:00, you can count on it!
16. I only go out with others who believe in themselves, have a good moral foundation, and respect me.
17. My life is too important to ruin it with tobacco. I don't like to smell like smoke, either.
18. I think more of myself and my friend than to be exposed to filthy language and scenes.
19. Sex is reserved for after marriage, period! One thing I'll never lose is my self-respect. If I don't respect me, no one else will either.
20. I accept who I am fully and completely. Some areas I can change (grades, teeth, weight, bad habits) but some I can't (height, race, color, ears, family, handicaps).

21. Others would like me if I were better at sports, better looking, smarter, richer, and so on.
22. I try to do most of the talking. That way people think I'm smart and outgoing.

23. I'd do anything to be popular.

24. I laugh at all jokes, if they are funny.
25. The "beat" is all that matters in my music.

26. I love to talk about others and to gossip.
27. I hate it when authority figures tell me what to do.

28. I never ask questions in class.

29. I never talk to my parents about my problems and concerns. They wouldn't understand, and I'd probably get in trouble.

30. My parents work full-time, and there is no one for me to talk to, so I often feel worthless and confused.

21. I realize the best way to make friends is to be a friend to others first.
22. I realize we have two ears and one mouth, so I try to listen more than I talk. Then others know I am truly interested in them and their thoughts.
23. I love being popular, but I will never compromise on my principles or beliefs. I know that if I don't stand for something, I will fall for anything.
24. If something or someone offends me, I never laugh.
25. I'm smart enough to know that damaging words and thoughts going into my mind will do me no good. (What goes in as words comes out as actions.)

26. I believe a simple phrase: "I will speak evil of no person."
27. I respect authority, even though I don't always agree with people.
28. If I've got a question, I always ask for the answer. If anyone makes fun of my "dumb" question, I figure it is his problem, not mine.
29. Even when I find it hard, I always try to talk to my parents about my concerns, problems, and fears. They have got their problems as well, so quite often I have to make the first move.
30. Though my family and I are very busy, I always find time to open up and share with special people in my life (my parents—when it is a convenient time—my coach, and other close friends).

How Did You Do?

25–30 positive = *I like me a lot.* You are doing really well. We'll work on the areas you need help on, and you will end up in great shape. Like an expensive race car, you need a little fine tuning.

18–25 positive = *I'm okay, but nothing great.* You look pretty good, but you can feel a lot better about yourself by working on your few negative areas. You have the capabilities of a Corvette if we get you some new tires (foundations) and put in some premium gas.

11–17 positive = *I'm not exactly my best friend.* You may feel you have a long way to go, but you are closer than you think to having a great self-esteem. Don't prepare for the junkyard yet. You do have some rust, which we will contend with in the upcoming pages.

0–11 positive = *I think of myself as that weirdo in the mirror.* You don't feel very happy with your life and probably don't think you have much hope for improvement. I'm here to tell you there is a huge amount of hope. Together we will bring you to a point where you feel proud of what you believe in and who you are. Just follow the simple map in the next pages.

Now that you've had a chance to look at your reactions to your own self-image, let's see what causes the trouble spots. We'll take a look at the things that keep us from being our best.

Self-image Destroyers

Two elements cause us to think poorly of ourselves:

> The unfair comparisons we make when we measure ourselves against others
> The negative beliefs others have fed us and we have put faith in

Either one can destroy your self-image, because each tells you that you are somehow not good enough. But you don't have to give in to such thought patterns. By becoming aware of how they work in your life, you can change how you think about yourself. Growing a good, healthy self-image will make you feel better about everything you do!

Unfair Comparisons

Unfair comparisons come in lots of shapes and sizes, but they all make you miserable. When you measure yourself by someone else's yardstick, you'll never come up with an accurate view of yourself. Every time you look at someone else and try to become as "perfect" as he or she seems, you'll end up falling on your face, because you will set unrealistic, impossible standards of perfection for yourself. But most of us have tried to live up to someone else's idea of what's good in these areas:

> Talents
> Physical beauty
> Intelligence
> Actions

What someone else thinks is good for him isn't necessarily right for *your* life. You'll need a clear view of yourself and your abilities before we move on, so let's see how this kind of thinking touches those four areas.

Talents. Have you ever thought something like *I'm so weak and skinny, and he's the big man on the wrestling team,* or, *I can't play the drums, and she's great at it?* When you do this, chances are you're concentrating on that other person's strong points and your weak ones—so of course you come up looking bad! It's like throwing a pair of loaded dice: You can't win.

Instead, when you think this way, realize that everyone has some talents, but no one has all of them. Maybe the wrestler feels so shy that he can't talk to anyone without getting tongue-tied. Or the girl who plays the drums just flunked math. In the same way, you don't have to be good in every area, just focus on the things you do well—and enjoy them.

Remember: Only compare *you* against what you *could be doing* or what you *could become.* Don't judge yourself by someone else's gifts.

Physical Beauty. Hollywood, I'm sick of it! Not everyone looks like your favorite movie star or model, so don't let your face or body stop you from making the most of your life. Phyllis Diller didn't try to look like the cover girls. She took her talent—humor—and made it into success. Jimmy Durante took his giant nose (a lemon) and turned it into lemonade.

When it comes to physical-beauty problems, I can really understand. My experience with them goes back a long way. When I was in second grade I saw a group of kids looking at me and giggling. Then the biggest one pointed his finger at me and said real loud, "Look at him. He's skinny." (He really had a way with words.) They saw my four most protruding features: my knobby knees and my bony elbows.

I went crying home from school, ran up to my dad, and said, "Da-Da-Dadd-Daddy [my bottom lip wouldn't stop quivering], they called me skinny." He looked down and said, "Well, you are skinny."

With that I went to my room and made a pact with myself that no one would ever again call me skinny (at least not because they saw my bony knees and elbows). I promised never to be seen in public in shorts or a short-sleeved shirt. Being a boy of my word, until I reached seventeen, I never wore such clothing. Can you imagine that? Seventeen years old before I had the confidence to let my elbows and knees publicly see daylight!

All those years I wore pants cut off or rolled up to just below my knees and shirts that covered my elbows. I figured that when others didn't see those parts of my anatomy, they'd think I had lots of muscles up there.

Today my story proves the importance of perception. I no longer call my physique skinny—now it's "trim and fit"!

Remember: Don't see yourself through Hollywood's eyes. Look at yourself in a positive way.

Intelligence. You'll know you've fallen into the intelligence-comparison trap when you think things like, *I'm not as smart as John in math, so I must not be as good a person,* or *Mary got a scholarship to a good college, and I missed out, so I'm a flop.* Making the most of your intelligence doesn't mean you have to be an Einstein. But you should do the most you can with the mental gifts you do have.

I never fooled anyone into thinking I was one of the smartest kids in my class. In fact I ranked in the part of the class that made the upper 50 percent possible. I even had bad breath. But since then I've learned that bad breath is better than no breath, and the lower half of the class is better than no education at all.

Remember: Each of us has special interests and abilities—this includes intellectual talents. Study hard in the areas you do well in, and others will see you as a highly intelligent person.

Actions. When you judge yourself against others' actions, it gets awful hard to look good. Because you couldn't get a part in the class play, you feel like a zero. Or because the teacher didn't mention your speech as the best one she's heard all year (but she did mention your friend's), you're a moron. Or you got cut from the team, so you're a klutz. If you fail one popularity poll, don't see yourself as a loser.

One year I went out for the football team (a stupid thing for a skinny kid to do). Because I didn't want to get my uniform dirty, I felt afraid to block anyone.

In the first game of the year I played defensive end. The first play of the game was an end-around run. That meant that everyone on the other team had one purpose in life for the next eight and a half seconds: TO KILL ME! My first glimpse of the immediate future came when I heard the offensive end—the fellow staring me in the eye—mention the word *kill*. As I saw the members of the other team run at me my mind began to work fast. Its short, sweet little talk went something like this: *Hey, turkey, you're gonna die!*

I responded the way any red-blooded, young, scared, wanting-to-be-popular-but-not-at-all-costs American kid would have: *I hit the dirt!* The guys on the other side ran right over me for the touchdown. That was my only play in organized football. The coach pulled me out of the game, and I quit the next week. Now, to encourage my self-esteem, someone labeled me Skinny Chicken Sanders.

No way could I believe that I had played my role well—and role playing is what our actions are all about. (I also learned something about a talent I *didn't* have.) If I'd believed that was the best job I'd ever do at anything, my self-esteem would have been as flat as my body was after two tons of football players finished digging their cleats into me. But I'm glad it didn't all end there.

Remember: Your identity should always rate a 9 or 10. Your role might deserve a 1 or −3, but that can't change your importance as a person. DON'T LET POOR PERFORMANCE LOWER YOUR PERCEPTION OF YOURSELF.

When you use any of these judgments on yourself, you're putting up impossible standards. If you think about it, you'll probably realize that no one else never fails at anything. It might seem that way, if you barely know a person and only see him during his good times, but even the football-playing, honor student who has all the girls in the class dying for a date with him has problems.

When I was in school, I wanted to be like the jocks. They seemed special. They had their own table in the cafeteria. They didn't eat like everyone else (they only used their bare hands). They didn't carry their books like the rest of the guys. These apes could take the biggest dictionary in the school and hold it down at one side, arm straight. When they took their giant steps, they grunted like Tarzan's jungle buddies.

Just once I wanted to be a jock and walk through the halls, hearing the girls sing "How Great Thou Art." Well, I never did, and I never will live up to my own impossible standard. You probably can't live up to some things you'd like to do, either. But you *can* live up to a higher goal than any you've probably ever thought about.

What's the solution to all these unfair-comparison problems? It's treating yourself as if you're *not* a monkey. Only Darwin's theory of evolution says we came from apes. If you realize that God created you just the way you are and stop blaming Him for everything you don't like in life, it will change your view of the world.

Almost everytime I go out to speak I meet people who have a healthy self-esteem as a direct result of their faith in God. I've heard people tell me things like: "If God made me, I'm gonna make something of myself for Him." "Now that I know I'm no mistake, I've got something to live for."

David Hartman of *Good Morning America*, has a positive self-image. He says his father told him one day, "Remember this, David: You are made in God's image, so you have His power in you. Who's going to waste that kind of power?"

I've never met a person who truly had a healthy self-esteem and peace of mind who didn't believe in God. Many people look or act successful on the outside, but they can't stand themselves on the inside. God helps you live with yourself and cope with this world.

As long as you blame God, you can't work with Him. When you start going in His direction, you'll soon discover some life goals you never imagined before. Suddenly a lot of things that never made sense will all fall into place—as long as you keep your eyes on Him. Don't fall for the damaging, devastating consequences that come with the view that you're no better than a monkey. Choose instead to think positively about your basic abilities and to make the most of what God has given you.

Negative Beliefs

Even when we don't compare ourselves to some ideal we could never live up to, we still have bad opinions of ourselves based on the thinking of other people:

> The negative things the world says to us
> The negative messages of the media
> The negative words others say to us
> The negative messages we get when people *don't* say something to us
> The negative reactions of others to our situation

What the World Says. We don't live in an upbeat world. Society gives us an opinion of ourselves that isn't very complimentary in most cases. If you don't have the latest clothes or the most expensive stereo system, you'll probably feel like an outcast, if you fall for this line. By trying to keep up with the constantly changing views of society, you'll drive yourself nuts!

When I tell you that seven out of ten people have negative attitudes, you'll begin to understand why our society acts so negative. We all seem to focus on the bad things in life more easily than we appreciate the good ones. At that rate it doesn't take long for everything to look pretty bleak.

Remember: Look for the positive. It's out there somewhere.

Media Messages. Every newscast tells about a tragedy. Books and magazines that describe the world today don't make it sound promising. Not many of them will help you attack the world's negative thinking. But some good, uplifting books, cassettes, television programs, and so on do exist. If you just turn on the boob tube and watch anything or listen to any radio show, without deciding what's good for you, you'll reflect the same attitude the media have. Give yourself something better!

Remember: As a young adult, you can only blame yourself for not putting good, clean, positive thoughts into your mind.

What Others Say. Anything someone else tells you about yourself you may believe more than your own opinion of yourself—especially if it's something negative. Even if that person is dead wrong, you can put faith in his words when he tells you you've been stupid, ugly, uncoordinated, or whatever. Somehow others always have more credibility to us than we do to ourselves.

Maybe that's why embarrassment seemed a permanent part of my younger years. I thought a lot of what others might think, and I always seemed to live up to their worst expectations. Like the time in the fourth grade when I made another of my graceful moves as a maturing young man.

Do you know what happens if you daydream with a pen in your mouth? Especially if you look at the pen and all the ink is gone? I felt my lip—ink on my finger, which had turned blue. I thought, *That's a weird place for ink.* [I didn't really think that—I just threw it in.] I *did* think: *No wonder you're so popular: You're always doing such cool things. I wonder if it's poisonous? I think I'm going to die!*

So I passed a note to my friend Kenny. It read: "Can I trust you with something real personal? I don't want to be embarrassed." He read it and whispered back to me, "Sure you can trust me. I'm your friend." I gave him a second note, which read: "I've got ink in my mouth. Find out if it's poisonous." He whispered back, "Don't worry, you can trust me. What are friends for anyway?" (Kenny was about to show me.) At the top of his lungs my pal shouted, "MRS. SMITH, BILL'S GOT INK IN HIS MOUTH. WILL HE DIE?"

I felt so embarrassed. I thought I *would* die as the class burst out laughing and I ran to the bathroom to wash my own mouth out with soap. They didn't even need to use words: That laughter spoke more clearly than any words my classmates could have spoken. *What a fool!*

You can try hard, but you'll never look perfect to everyone. If you don't make a mistake all on your own, occasionally someone will help you to one. Plenty of people will gladly think bad thoughts about you, too (remember the seven out of ten). If you let it bother you, you'll just wear yourself out keeping track of them. Don't take it too seriously.

Remember: Some people find fault as though there were a reward for it.

When People Don't Say Something. At times you may find yourself waiting for others to praise you or give you accepting nods. If your friends or family or teachers don't notice you, you feel they don't care.

While you wait for such boosts for your ego, bring along plenty of camping equipment—you'll stay in the same place for a long time. So when the provisions run out and you decide to pull down the tent, try something that works better: Take responsibility for becoming your own encourager and best friend. Give yourself rewards when you do something that makes you proud of yourself. Don't wait for the world to notice your accomplishments. If you don't develop habits of loving and comforting yourself, you'll grow up into a lonely adult.

Just because you don't have a lot of support and help, don't think you can't make it. If no one's pulling for you, listen to this story.

When she was a child, she only wanted to become an actress. At eighteen she went from her home in upper New York State, to New York City, where she enrolled in a well-acclaimed acting school. After three months of hard work and total dedication, the school sent her mother a letter. It read, "Our school has produced some of the greatest actors and actresses the United States, and even the world, has ever known. However, we have never had a student with less talent and ability than your daughter. She is no longer enrolled in our school."

What a shock! A lifetime of dreams and wants could have been totally ruined by one letter, but not for this determined girl. Being kicked out of school and told she was worthless only made her more determined.

For the next two years she took all sorts of jobs to earn enough money to live on. She applied at almost every tryout that came along. She always heard the same thing, "You will never become an actress. You have no talent or ability!"

This aspiring actress came down with a severe case of pneumonia that so weakened her legs that the doctors told her she would never walk again. How do you react to this terrible situation? Not only won't anyone support your desire to act, but now you can't walk. She worked with weights on each leg, and after two long and painful years of therapy, she could walk. She had a limp, but she worked hard to conceal it.

At age twenty-one she returned to New York City to try again. Guess what? She was turned down for eighteen years. That's right—eighteen years! When she was forty years old she got her first substantial acting job. Was it worth it? To her it was. In 1953 over 40 million people watched her television special. Her name? Lucille Ball. She wasn't born talented or great or beautiful. She had no breaks, and she didn't know important people, but she stuck to it. Stick to your dreams and desires, and you too can walk tall and proud.

Remember: You need to be your own coach and encourager.

Reactions of Others. If you have a problem with something in your life—your family situation, past, color, or a physical handicap—it gets easy to put the blame elsewhere: "My family is poor and uneducated, so I'll always be like them." "I've been a loser all my life—I can't change now." "It's my race [or color] that holds me back." "If I hadn't had that accident as a kid, it'd be different." The excuses are endless, but you don't have to give in to them.

When your situation seems unbearable, and you feel you can't go a step farther, think about Joni (it's pronounced *Johnny*). As a teen, this girl had everything going for her—athletic ability, popularity, faith in God—life seemed great. Then a diving accident left her paralyzed—a quadriplegic. But that's not the end of Joni's story. Instead of letting her situation control her, she let God control her life. As a result, she really has something to share: a story of overcoming huge odds and turning her handicap into something to glorify Him. She has appeared on Billy Graham's crusades, as well as almost every other major Christian TV show, radio show, and any other place where she could share her faith. Joni has written books, she sings songs and counsels with other handicapped people. Because she knows what it is to go through pain and suffering, she gives hope, love and encouragement to those who hurt.

If you find yourself down and hurting, help someone less fortunate, and watch your own situation improve.

Remember: The history books are filled with great people from every walk of life, every color and creed, and every possible awful situation.

Fighting Back

How many of the image destroyers and negative beliefs have gotten to you? Everyone has fallen into such traps at one time or another, and just because you know what one feels like doesn't mean you have a major problem in that area. Pick out the ones you experience most often. Now that you're aware of them, make positive efforts to change your wrong thinking. The next chapter will show you how.

When you start to put some of these steps into action, like the teen who wrote me this letter, you'll have a better opinion of yourself:

> I never thought it was possible to believe in myself. After I heard you speak and say how special and unique I was I started to believe it. Now everything I do is different. I believe in ME!

Check Out Your Turf

1. If you haven't tested your self-esteem, go back to the SEQ test and answer all the questions. Now take a look at the answers. What are your biggest strong points? What are your biggest weak points?

2. Which of your weak points in your self-esteem result from unfair comparisons? from negative beliefs fed to you by others? Who have you compared yourself to? Who has told you you didn't measure up?

3. How have you made unfair comparisons in your talents? physical beauty? intelligence? actions? Why are such standards impossible to achieve? How can you start treating yourself as if you're not a monkey?

4. What negative messages have you believed in? Why are they wrong? How can you start fighting back?

3

BUILDING A POSITIVE SELF-IMAGE

Now that we've looked at the need for improvement, let's see what we can do about building a self-image that really works. I'd like to share with you thirteen steps to becoming your own best friend.

Step 1: Realize That You Didn't Come From a Monkey! Recognize and develop strength in the facts that God created you and that He cannot make mistakes. *You are no mistake.* God doesn't make junk!

I always felt mad at God for not making me good at sports or muscular or a fast runner. *Why,* I wondered, *did he make me tall and skinny?* Sure I could talk fairly well, but that didn't ease the pain or the anger I felt at being a physical misfit. I failed to see that God made me tall and thin and able to speak because he had other plans for me: a professional speaking career. He knew all along what I would do for a livelihood. If you are not totally happy with yourself (and I know you probably aren't), put yourself back on God's easel and let Him work on you some more. Remember these letters: PBPWMGINFWMY. They stand for, "Please Be Patient With Me, God Is Not Finished With Me Yet."

Step 2: Don't Compare Yourself With Others. Compare you with you. Do you realize that if you were the only person in the world, you might feel lonely, but you would probably have a healthy self-esteem? If you didn't look around at others in school and see kids who seemed better looking, richer, happier, more coordinated, you wouldn't see yourself in a negative light. Picture this: Three sisters who are triplets. All three are the prettiest in the entire school. All the other girls envy their beauty, but all three are the most unhappy girls in their class. Why? Because they compare themselves with each other. Each one thinks the other two look better, so they all feel miserable. What a shame!

If you compare yourself with others, try this. Engage in *positive comparison*. Look at positive qualities, characteristics, or learned skills in others and use them to challenge yourself. Only look at areas in your life that you can change. You can't compare looks; we can't do much to change our looks. You can't compare family background or height; we can't change those, either. But you can desire another's dedication to practice, his honesty and respect for others, or her developed memory (by the way, each of us has a great memory. It is either trained or untrained. So if you forget something just say, "It's my memory—it's untrained").

Step 3: Become Really Good at Something. Find your "thing," do it, and do it well. People who believe in themselves and can hold their heads high and look others in the eye almost always have their "specialty." They've become really good at something, and—*it doesn't matter what it is!* Ask yourself, *What am I good at? What skills seem to come naturally? What am I willing to work hard at and practice over and over? What would I like to excel in?* Find your song and sing it. Please believe me when I say this. *Greatness lives in you!* I absolutely believe it. Say it to yourself over and over again: *There* *is greatness in me. I will become really good at _____."*

You see, the real winners of a marathon are those who gave it their best—their all. A friend of mine came in 124 out of over 300 runners in a marathon. That means 123 people came in before him, but he felt like a winner. He stood at the finish line and congratulated the rest of the runners who came in after him. He says, "I compete against me, no one else. I ran my race today, and I'm proud that I finished and did my best."

My nephew Andy wasn't muscular and athletic like his cousins, whom he was very close to. For the first years of his life this bothered him, and he really didn't think much of himself. When he entered high school, he became interested in two hobbies. By practicing and spending many hours he became the best he could. Today he plays the trumpet better than anyone else in his entire school. He is also an accomplished bird watcher. He has made positive identification of more birds in his state of Ohio than 95 percent of the people his age. Andy now has self-esteem. He believes in himself. He didn't worry about what he couldn't do, but went ahead and became really good at two things that lie within his interests. You can find your areas also.

Step 4: Develop a Well-Rounded Life. Life is made up of six main areas: family, spiritual, mental, social, physical and financial. As you can see in Illustration 1, our lives are designed to center around the spiritual part. That's why Step 1 in building

Illustration 1

a healthy self-concept of ourselves is to realize that God created us. When we get right with our Maker, it becomes much easier to get the rest of our lives in order. A person who's not well rounded might look like Illustration 2. This person has put way too much emphasis on social (popularity) and financial (material things). No wonder he might not believe in himself. He's out of balance.

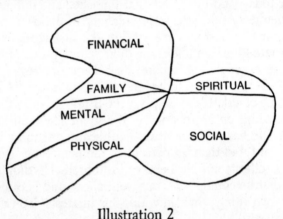

Illustration 2

Step 5: Learn How to Be Motivated From Within. What you tell yourself about yourself has a lot to do with how well motivated you'll feel. Without even realizing it, you give yourself messages about how you're doing—whether you're a winner or a loser. Psychologists call this unconscious conversation with yourself self-talk.

You can control the thoughts you feed yourself—what you think about *is* up to you. Instead of focusing on the negative, turn to the positive.

NEGATIVE SELF-TALK	POSITIVE SELF-TALK
I can't do it.	*I can do it. I know I can.*
I knew I'd flunk that test.	*That test score wasn't like me. I'm a winner. I'll do better next time.*
I'll never get picked for the lead part in the play.	*I can see it now: Opening night— I'm the lead part, and it goes great.*

That's just my luck. Things never go right for me.

I didn't do as well as I can, but I'll do better next time.

Why is everyone looking at me? I bet my pants are unzipped.

People always look at me. It must be my new haircut. I knew they would like it.

Don't listen to the negative voices of the world around you.

IF THE WORLD SAYS	YOU SAY
(*A student in the hall*) "Another lousy Monday."	"Monday is just a day. It is not lousy or good. We make it good. I think I will have a super, fantastic, good day today."
(*The weatherperson*) "There is a sixty percent chance of rain today."	"There is a forty percent chance of sunshine today."
(*Your friend*) "If I don't get asked out for that date, I'll just die."	"I think I know your problem. You've been saying that for so long—he thinks you're dead!
"Look at that stop light."	"It's a 'go light.'"
"I love the weekend."	"Not me—I love the 'strong end.'"
(*A kid in the cafeteria*) "I don't want the 'end' of that bread."	"Every loaf of bread I see has two 'beginnings.'"
(*Your brother*) "I've got a 'cold.'"	"I don't believe in colds. I did catch a slight 'warm' last winter."
(*A teacher*) "This is the toughest test you'll have all year."	"I like challenges. I will study extra hard and make it easy."
(*A smart aleck at school*) "I'm going to make more money than you this summer."	"Not unless you get a job in a mint. That's the only place people 'make' money. The rest of us earn it."
"Where do you live?" "Is it a long walk?"	"The corner of walk and don't walk." "If the light gets stuck."
"How far is it from your house to my house?"	"The same distance it is from my house to your house."

This week try noticing how most people respond with negative actions, words, and expectations. But don't let yourself get caught up with the rest of these negatrons. Remember: Words are motivators moving us toward success or failure. If you let other people's negativisms affect you, you'll fall back into failure. Go ahead and feel sorry for them, but don't follow their example.

Most of all, don't let yourself be caught up in such senseless negative attitudes and actions as I did in my junior year of high school.

One day as I walked down the hall in school, minding my own business, the unexpected happened: a Mack truck hit me, and I fell to the ground with the laughter of my classmates ringing in my ears. Well, it wasn't really a Mack truck, but another student. Because he had been running behind me, I had no clue of what would happen until his large hand hit me with great force. Extending his arm and putting his full weight behind the shove, he had toppled me over effortlessly. Picking myself up, I felt embarrassed and angry, yet I didn't have enough nerve to fight back. That didn't mean I forgot him, though; for the next two years I made it my goal to *kill* him. Preferably, in front of the entire student body—on video for the entire world to see.

In preparation I began to get in shape. I ordered a muscle-man outfit with giant horse pills, a book on becoming another Atlas, and two dumbbells. Guess who was really the dumbbell? I also enrolled in a karate class and worked for almost a year and a half to attain new heights of glory. No one ever knew about my secret goal of beating him up in front of everyone, but it kept burning inside me just the same. (I still can't believe that I spent a year and a half of my life with one consuming aim—to get even. It was probably the biggest waste of time, and the most senseless ambition I've had. Getting even just puts you on the same wavelength and level as the person you feel angry at. It also shows you cannot control your own emotions. I let someone else totally control me, what I thought about, and how I acted. He had forgotten the incident five minutes later, but with me it lasted a year and a half. How stupid.)

Step 6: Look Your Best at All Times. People who are "dressed up" feel up. You don't have to have the most expensive clothes. Just be clean and neat. Your attitude changes when people say, "You look nice," or, "I like that sweater."

Step 7: Read Good Books and Listen to Motivating Cassettes. Good biographies and autobiographies can help you learn from other's successes. Read about famous leaders in all areas of life, especially those who had well-rounded lives. Notice how some famous people never did well in one area. By studying others, you can see where you want to be strong and not make the same mistakes. Listen to cassettes that will motivate you and help you believe in yourself and set new goals. Listen to teachers and speakers with positive, uplifting messages. Even boring speakers have good points if you will listen for them and pick them out.

After my junior year in college I read my first book, cover to cover. That's right. All through school I never read an entire book. I associated reading books with bookworms, and I didn't want to be a bookworm. One day I picked up a book by Dale Carnegie called *How to Win Friends and Influence People*, and for the first time in my life I began to hear the same type of things that I am sharing with you now: that life is a cause-and-effect situation. What we do causes an effect. What we give out comes back. I read that if you smile, most people will smile back. I learned that if you plant corn, you can't get beans. If you plant good thoughts in your mind, bad actions for the most part will not come out. In the same way, when you plant bad thoughts over and over, good actions will not come out.

I got so excited that I called the local Dale Carnegie people, and a salesman came and signed me up for the next course. Though it cost several hundred dollars, and I didn't know anything about it, I felt very excited.

In this fourteen-week, public-speaking class, they get people on their feet to give short talks in front of the other class members, to help build self-confidence. During the fifth session, I got the best-speech award of the night. I even received a standing ovation. Two days later, from the man who signed me up, Don Davies, I received a card. It said, "In all my years with Dale Carnegie, I have never seen a standing ovation at anything other than a graduation ceremony. You have some kind of speaking talent in you. Keep it up. You will go a long ways." The next week I felt afraid to go back, because I had an image to live up to, so I quit the class. That's right—I quit! I didn't have a fear of *failure*. Like many people, I had a fear of success. *How can I outdo what I did before?* I asked myself. *If I do well, they will expect more from me. If I try my best now, they will think I can always do it.* Do you know what? Mr. Davies kept calling me for almost a year and convinced me to go back and take the course again. He kept telling me I had a speaking talent. Even though I didn't believe him, I started the course again, a year later, just to get him off my back. This time I showed him that he had someone to believe in. I proved to him that all his effort had a purpose and a reason, because this time I didn't quit the course until the seventh session. That's right. After the seventh session I felt so afraid to get up there and speak that I quit again. The days I had a class I became nervous. I couldn't eat all day, because I was so afraid of that two-minute speech. But do you know what he had the nerve to do? He called me up the very next day and said, "You're going to take it again. You are going to finish this thing."

Well, about three weeks later, in a neighboring town, because of his persistence and his belief in me, I took the class. I finished the course this time. I even ended up being an assistant in several other classes, and I sold the Dale Carnegie course for two years. It turned into one of the greatest, self-confidence builders in my life.

A year or so later I got ahold of some motivational cassette tapes. The first one was called *The Strangest Secret*, by Earl Nightingale. He simply states that the strangest thing in the world is that we become what we think about. Solomon says,

"As a man thinketh in his heart, he becomes" (*see* Proverbs 23:7). If I think about success, I will become successful. If I think about failure, I will become a failure. If I think I will get good grades and picture in my mind getting good grades, most likely I will work hard and fulfill that vision. I shared these cassettes with some friends, and before I knew it, several people were getting together on a regular basis to hear them. One day a friend of mine named Bill had an idea. He said, "Wouldn't it be something if we could have fifty or sixty people get together and listen to these and all grow and become more positive and successful?" We rented a large hockey stadium and hired seven other speakers. The greatest salesman in the world, Joe Girard, spoke. One of the most exciting female speakers ever to grace the platform, Marilyn Van Derbur, was there. Robert Schuller from the Crystal Cathedral, Wayne Dyer, who wrote *Your Erroneous Zones*, Earl Nightingale himself, Art Fettig (called Mr. Lucky), Dr. Denis Waitley, the psychology of winning expert, my friend Bill, and myself. Bill acted as MC that day, and I spoke on the platform with everyone else. I felt scared to death. Of course, the real amazing thing came in the fact that we sold over 6,000 tickets in our little town for this marvelous event. We found out a month later that a large rally like this had never been attempted in a town with smaller than 1 million population. Our town only has 100,000 in it, but you see what happened. We became what we thought about. We pictured success, and we went after it, and we just happened to get it. We were like the bumblebee. It does not know that it cannot fly—it just flies. Do you know that scientists have it proven scientifically and aerodynamically that it is impossible for the bumblebee to fly? Guess why it can do it? It doesn't bother reading their books; it just flies.

About halfway through the promotion of that rally, we met a man named Dale Maloney. He showed us that we could do it, because he had done it before. He showed us creative ways of selling tickets, of knocking on doors and talking to people and using enthusiasm. He got my younger brother, Dale, so excited that he went for a Guinness world record. He wanted to make the most telephone calls in a one-month period. Even though he didn't get the record, he personally sold over 2,000 tickets.

My talk that day was entitled, "Find Your Song and Sing It." I wanted everyone to know that life was meant to be lived. There is a song in each one of us that needs to be sung. We need to shout it to the highest treetops. I also shared that day how my new courage to stand on that stage and to do one of the most frightful things of giving a speech entirely resulted from an action I had taken four months earlier, when I invited Jesus into my life. I felt afraid to share that. Many people even advised me not to, because I might turn the crowd off, but I just had to. It burst within me. I couldn't hold it back. Do you know what happened? Right in the middle of my speech, I received a beautiful, loud applause. They, too, admired my stand. By the way, from that talk, I received over thirty invitations to speak within the next month. I believe that was just a manifestation of my standing up for what I believed in.

Since that time, I have had the opportunity and blessing of sharing the platform with such notable speakers as Paul Harvey, Art Linkletter, Zig Ziglar, Dr. Norman Vincent Peale, President Ford and President Reagan. Many thousands of young people all across the country have delighted me as I have shared the message that meant so much to me. I have made several cassettes myself. One of my greatest joys is my six-cassette album entitled *The Student's Guide to Earning Money*, produced by the Nightingale Conant Corporation.

It all started when I read one book and listened to one cassette.

Step 8: Try Something New Each Week! Each week step out of your "comfort zone." Once you get into the habit of trying new things, your confidence level will grow by leaps and bounds.

Try one of these each week:

    A. Introduce yourself to someone new.
    B. Write someone a thank-you or I-was-just-think-
       ing-of-you note.

C. Ask at least one question per class. (Make sure it's a question that is on your mind. Don't just ask a nonsense question because I've suggested it.)

D. If the opportunity arises, give an oral book report instead of a written one.

E. Always look for opportunities to give a report, help take attendance, give a short speech, and so on. (The greatest single confidence-building activity I know of is public speaking. You won't be perfect, but you will be one of the top 5 percent in your class when you give it a try!) Others will admire your courage. Don't say you feel nervous, and no one will know.

F. Stop to help another student (if he has just dropped his books, can't get his locker opened, needs help carrying something, or needs someone to talk to).

G. Sit next to different people in the cafeteria. Others will start to notice you have more courage than they do. This will give you courage to keep growing.

H. Ask the teacher for extra work to do in areas you enjoy. (By the way, this is not apple polishing. You are developing the attitude of doing more than expected. When you get in the job market, you will earn more than expected also.)

I. Look for a frown on another student's face and be her friend. (Find a frown and turn it upside down.)

J. Help a lower classperson, or just be nice to him. (Remember: What you give away to others comes back to you also.)

K. Tell your mom and dad you love them and need to have some time alone with them to talk.

L. This one may give you heart failure, but try it anyway. Be nice to your younger brother or sister. Specifically ask if you can help on a project or with homework. (I told you it may cause serious health problems.)

M. Organize a homework night for three or four students who don't know the material as well as you do. This will be good leadership practice for you.

N. If you're old enough to take on a job, write a letter to a local business, asking to have an interview concerning summer employment.

The summer I was seventeen, I tried something new: My friend Steve and I painted our way to California and back. We did the yellow lines on parking lots the whole way. We set a goal of $200.00 a day—or we wouldn't sleep. We would knock on doors, ask for the job, and then we would open the trunk, get our materials, and paint the lines on the parking lot. Always we guaranteed satisfaction—except one time in Denver. After we had completed the job as the lady had asked, she came out and said, "Repaint it. I want all the lines to go a different way." We went across the street to get some black paint, so we could black out the old yellow lines and repaint it. The man told us, "I saw her arguing with you. She gives everyone a hard time. Do you want to have some fun?" We said, "Sure." Handing us some cans, he replied, "Here is some paint that will last until the first rain. Give it a try." We didn't know about integrity in business, so we went ahead and gave it a try. We blacked out the old lines and painted the new, and she gave us our money. A week later, on a rainy day, we drove out of town, passing by that lot. It was the funniest thing you ever saw: lines going every which way. Though I'm ashamed of it now, we had a good laugh as we rode off.

For the next three summers I painted parking lots. It helped pay for a lot of my college education. Most of all, it gave me an identity. I came back to school with a new car. People didn't notice my car so much, but they did notice me walking taller. For the first time in my life I could do something that other kids couldn't do. I learned how to earn money. That is why I encourage you to find something that you can do and do well. Discover your burning desire inside.

Now make a list of your own. The important thing is not

how well you do in these activities but that you give them a try. You probably will find some unexpected things you really do well at. Go ahead, no one will develop your self-confidence for you. Winners and positive people pay the price by doing the things most others hate to do. Make that list.

Step 9: Save Money! Save at least 10 percent of every dollar you earn—preferably 20 percent. Living at home, you can do it. A friend of mine saved several thousand dollars from his paper route, in about five years. After high school he bought a house with his money. He had a better self-image just knowing he was able to save money while all his friends "blew" the money they had. I know, I always spent my money on the first thing that came along.

Step 10: Make a Blessed List and a Success List. A blessed list describes the abilities and talents and things you have been given without hard work and effort. A success list shows achievements you have accomplished because of hard work and effort.

Step A: Take a three-by-five card.

Step B: Put twenty things in each column.

For example:

MY BLESSED LIST	MY SUCCESS LIST
1. A great family	1. I learned to talk
2. A loving dad	2. I learned to walk
3. A dedicated mom	3. I can tie my shoes
4. My church	4. Hop
5. My eyesight	5. Ride a bike
6. My legs	6. Read
7. My ability to hear	7. Read *Treasure Island*
8. My heart	8. Boy/Girl Scouts (all accom-
9. My overall health	plishments)
10. Living in America	9. Learned to drive
11. Freedom of choice	10 Built a model airplane
12. My school	11. Baked a cake
13. My many freedoms	12. Ate the cake [just kidding]
14. Wise authorities in my life	13. Good friendship with Mary
15. My sports ability	14. Quit complaining about get-
16. My good looks	ting up early

17. My singing talent
18. Sense of humor
19. Love for people
20. God's love for me

15. Stopped smoking
16. Lost five pounds
17. Got an *A* in English
18. Said no to drugs
19. Came home on time all last year [okay, one month]
20. My savings account

Note: Your successes should be from all ages of your life. They don't have to be giant, world-shaking accomplishments. These will remind you of the effort you put forth in the past and give you hope for achieving more now.

Step C: Put a goal (something you really want to accomplish) on the other side. Make it a goal that you can accomplish in one month.
For example:

My Goal:
I will lose five pounds by [one month from today]
Date

Sign your name

Step D: Fold the card in half three or four times. It will now be small enough to put into your pocket. Carry it everywhere you go for thirty days. Read it first thing in the morning and last thing at night. If you think of more blessings or successes, add them to the lists. You will focus on the great things in your life, instead of the problem areas. You will begin to have greater belief in your ability to control your life. This will help you:

Practice your positive self-talk
Step out of your comfort zones
Become really good at something
Look your best in front of others
Save money
Compare inner qualities instead of outward appearances

In short: this one little activity will help you become more self-confident, raise your self-esteem, believe in yourself more, say no to peer pressure, rise above the crowd, become your best, and try harder to be better. Go to it! I know you can do it!

Step 11: Smile, Look People in the Eyes, Be a Great Listener, and Learn to Say Thank You! These four simple yet seldom-used activities will automatically put you on the trail toward a healthier self-esteem and more confidence.

When you smile, you look happy. Others think you are happy, so they act happy around you. This chain reaction gives you even more reasons to smile.

By looking people in the eyes you will feel better about yourself and tuned into them as well.

By becoming a great listener, you will be the person more people want to be around. More people equals more friends, which leads to popularity. This in turn, helps you like yourself better.

When someone gives you a compliment, don't apologize! Say thanks! For example: "I like your new coat." Say, "Thanks." Don't say, "Oh, it's nothing. I have another one that looks better. I just happened to grab this one at the last minute. It doesn't really fit well, either."

Step 12: Avoid These Destructive Elements at All Costs:

A. *Avoid pornography!* If you see people at their worst, your value as a person will also go downhill. (Remember: The people who manufacture, promote, and sell pornography love your money but don't care a bit about your self-image.)

B. *Avoid believing in the "science" of astrology.* People who read and believe in their horoscopes believe life is based on "luck" or "chance." They fail to realize that their *actions cause the outcomes* in their lives. Tell people dedicated to their "sign" that astrology was founded on the assumption that the sun revolves around the earth.

C. *Avoid daytime and nighttime soap operas* Life is not that negative for people who apply the principles of this book. What goes into your mind turns to thoughts, which leads to actions and later on to habits. If you don't want to have a life of misery and heartache, then don't study those who are good at it.

Step 13: Choose the Right Friends. Follow these simple rules:

A. Never "hang around" and choose for your best friends people who would encourage you to do something you would feel ashamed to do in front of your parents or God.

B. Never date anyone you wouldn't marry.

C. Girls, if a guy ever says, "If you love me you'll go all the way," don't walk out on him. First spit in his face, and then *run* out on him!

Please believe me. I don't want any of this to sound like I am preaching at you. I deeply care about your life and the way you live it. I made many wrong choices all through my teen years. I never knew who were my "friends" and who weren't. My self-image wasn't high enough to say no to the wrong activities or people. This little piece on friendship may help express my feelings on the importance of discovering your "true friends."

Friendship isn't easy.
It isn't hard either, but it *is* commitment.
It says, I'll stand up for you.
I'll never talk behind your back.
And I'll only help you believe in you,
because you believe in me.
I'll never tear you down
or laugh at your mistakes.
Encouragement is all you'll ever receive from me.
And long after we graduate from school
I'll still keep in touch.
I'll pray for you and wish you the best.
I'll spend time at your house and invite you to mine.

I'll want everyone to meet you,
because I'm proud to be your friend.
I'll brag on you when I'm with others.
You see, it's easy to do these things.
After all, that's what friendship is all about.

I dedicate this to Steve McKinley. A friend who has always "been there" for me.

That summer Steve and I took our trip to California, a magnificent thing happened in Colorado. While we painted a parking lot on a hot August day, Steve said to me, "Take your shirt off and get some sun." Of course I never told him or anyone else why I didn't wear short-sleeved shirts or short pants, but he knew just the same. As I told him, "No, it's okay. I'm not that hot," he replied, "Hey, listen, we're friends. Don't you know it's what's on the inside that counts? I don't care if you are a muscle man or how smart you are. We happen to be friends, and that's that. Now get your shirt off."

That day broke the barrier. It became all right for me, for the first time in a long time, to be me. My parents had told me all my life that I was special and unique, that I had talents, and that I should use them. My teachers said the same thing. Of course, I didn't believe them. My parents *had* to say that. I knew the teachers got paid for that job. But now a friend, one whom I admired and looked up to, told me it was okay to be me. I guess the old saying is true: "When the student is ready, the teacher appears."

Friends can influence you in many ways—good or bad ones. So be careful whom you choose to influence your life.

Well, there you have it. You aren't born believing in yourself or not believing in you. Self-image doesn't depend on luck or the location where you live. It comes in all sizes, shapes, and colors. It means deciding on what you choose to believe in and stand for. Let's compare it to taking a ride in a car. First you get dressed. Then you get the keys, unlock the car, put your seatbelt on [by the way, you will surely be one of the weirdos if you wear your seatbelt—you also may be one of the live ones, too], turn on the car, look both ways, back up, and then drive away. To the fourteen-year-old wanting to drive, it all looks easy. But the driver knows of the many unseen steps to actually taking a ride in the car.

In the same way believing in yourself has hidden steps. Follow the ones I've told you about. They do work! They have worked for me and a million others. Right now many students in your school and town are using them to build success.

You may see yourself as a pile of lumber. Together, one step at a time, you and I will build a wonderful castle out of this heap.

You may see yourself as an old bicycle tire. The spokes are loose and it wobbles like crazy. Together we will tighten the right areas and turn your life into a well-rounded, smooth-rolling machine.

Check Out Your Turf

1. Which areas of your life (spiritual, financial, family, social, mental, physical) need work? Which are your strongest? List some things you would like to accomplish in each area and a date by which you hope to see some results. Try to think of some specific goals that will help you see your growth. (Vague goals will only frustrate you, because you won't know when you've achieved them.) Be realistic in how much you can accomplish, but don't be *too* easy on yourself, either.
2. How have you used negative self-talk? positive self-talk? How have they affected your life? Can you start to change today? List some ways.
3. If you haven't already, make a Blessed and Success List. Share some of your blessings with a friend or family member and ask that person how he or she has been blessed.
4. What other steps listed in this chapter do you need to take? When can you realistically expect to accomplish them?

FROM THE BOTTOM UP (BUILDING LIFE ON THE RIGHT FOUNDATION)

If you're like most folks, you look at people and try to figure whether or not they are happy. You see someone laughing and having fun and say to yourself, *He doesn't have any problems. I bet everything goes good for him.* Or that most popular person gives the impression she is set for life. In this chapter let's look at people who not only look happy on the outside, but feel contented on the inside.

Such people find their peace in the foundation they stand on—and I don't mean what kind of shoes they wear. I mean what they stake their lives on. What is important enough to fight or stand up for?

Look at the Foundation

No matter what you mention—a building, a tree, a life, or a country—*the foundation will tell how long it will stand.* If the foundation is sturdy and secure, it will last and pass the test of time. If not, it will crash to the ground!

When Holly and I went camping in California, we visited Yosemite National Park, the home of the Giant Sequoias. They say one tree has enough wood in it to build thirty inexpensive homes. To me those trees represented the popular students in my school. Everyone talks about them, they are the center of attention and everyone admires their vast beauty.

I asked the guide taking us through the park how deep the roots went on those giants. I figured they must go down several hundred feet—maybe even a thousand. He told me, "Eight to fifteen feet." I asked, "That's all? How do they stand up under the winds and storms?" He replied, "Everyone is amazed when they first hear how shallow the roots are. But they don't realize how far out they travel in all directions. Thousands and thousands of feet. It's like millions of little hands and arms holding tight to get water and secure a grip to hold those beautiful things in the air." He also told me it would be better if they went deeper. Quite often smaller trees with deeper roots stay standing while some of the huge redwoods topple to the ground under heavy winds.

In the construction business, those in charge know that their buildings must have the right foundations in order to hold the structures' weight and support them. Experienced architects can tell you how tall a building is going to be by looking at the hole in the ground. They know exactly how much weight the concrete base can hold.

Great civilizations, too, need the right base. Studies show that world powers such as America last about two hundred years. From all that I have read and from the experts I have heard, the family and what it stands for and believes in forms the cornerstone of a country or nation. When the family fails, so does the nation. I believe America is too young to die, but I am also smart enough to look around and see the shape of our family structure. If some changes don't come about, as a world power, we too will become history. We wisely need to look at our past, see what made us strong in the first place, and go back to it. I like what Paul Harvey said in his recording, *The Uncommon Man.*

> Men and women came here [to the United States] in the first place, not to be free to do what they wanted, but to *be free to do what they ought.* America is not a way of worship . . . it's a place of worship. When nations turn from God to worship idols, He lets them.

He also says that today, more than ever, such little effort produces giant results. A little enthusiasm can catapult you to great heights, and the mature young person realizes that honest hard work and effort almost always make up for a lack of genius and talent.

What About You?

How deep do your roots go? How firmly have you built your foundation? If you want to play the piano well, how deep have your practice roots traveled? How many times have you given that speech or run for a class office?

What you do, plan for, and prepare for now will determine what the future holds for you. You construct your foundation out of what you stand *on* and *for.* Don't excuse yourself with the idea that you're a teenager and no normal teen spends time thinking about things like this. I know 95 percent of your peers don't work on this or give it five minutes' a month thought, but *you* are not 95 percent of the people your age. *You* are different. Did you know that by reading this book you will automatically be in the upper 10 percent of the people in our country? That's right. Studies show that less than 10 percent of Americans read at least one book a year. By doing that alone, you have become unique.

Let's look at the four major foundations that your life stands on. If these areas are weak, so will your life be. If they are strong, you as a person will also be strong.

No matter what endeavor we want to be successful at, it's wise to study the greats who have gone on before us. If we wanted to look at swimmers, we would at least have to include Mark Spitz. He won seven Olympic gold medals in 1972. Before him, no one accomplished that. If you wanted to compose music, you would be wise to study Mozart and Beethoven. Then you'd learn from *OPE*: "Other People's Experience." Why invent the wheel over and over again? Study how it's been done before and improve on that.

I wanted to use as our example a person who has been written about and admired by more people than anyone else since the beginning of time—someone who could give us the true meaning of happiness and success. If we build our life on the important things He has shown us, we could truly live and like ourselves more. The one I'm thinking of happens to be my hero. I hope, whether or not you believe in Him, you will at least look closely at the four main foundations He stood on.

Only one sentence in all of His book describes Him as a teenager. By the way, His book has sold more copies than any other book ever printed. Famous men and women have said for years that if they were confined to prison for life and could only take one book with them, it would be this book. The book of course is the Bible, and the teen is Jesus of Nazareth. In Luke 2:52 the sentence reads, "And Jesus increased in *wisdom*, and *stature*, and in favour with *God* and *man*" (*italics mine*).

Area 1: Wisdom—But I Ain't No Einstein

What is wisdom? Why would I want to be wise?—even if I knew what it took. People have called me a wiseacre, but I don't think that counts.

Wisdom means "knowledge guided by understanding." It has to do with knowing right from wrong and differentiating the good ideas from the bad ones. We gain wisdom by improving our minds, our mental strength, reading, learning from our mistakes and victories, listening to other wise people, watching others succeed or fail, and from being attentive at school, in church, and at assemblies.

What goes into your mind comes out. If nothing goes in (no reading or learning) nothing can come out. The computer world calls it GIGO: "Garbage in, garbage out."

Study. Make the most of your classes. Time goes faster when you are prepared and ready for tests, especially if you plan to further your education after high school. Develop good study habits *now!* Even as I write this chapter, I learn the importance of diligent study while all alone. All the great people of the past have spent time alone, preparing and practicing their art. Beethoven used to rise at daybreak and, without food, go straight to his piano and compose until two or three in the afternoon. Tom Watson hits over 500 golf balls a day. Wilma Rudolph (the only woman to win three Olympic gold medals) used to sneak out of her dorm room and run from 10:00 P.M. until early morning. She would then get up and go to class with everyone else. Thomas Edison would go for days without sleep, working on his experiments and inventions. That doesn't mean sleep is bad. You need a good night's rest, but you *will* have to sacrifice for your goals.

The Classic Example of Wisdom. Let's see wisdom at work. History has recorded King Solomon as one of the wisest men who lived. God told him, "Ask whatever you wish me to give you." Instead of money, fame, fortune, or a long life, he asked for an understanding heart—one that can tell between good and evil. He knew he needed wisdom.

Two women came to the king, both claiming a certain little child was theirs. Each maintained the other lied. Solomon commanded, "Take a sword and divide the child in two. Half for each." One woman cried, "No, don't kill him. Let her have him." The other said, "Divide him. Neither of us shall have him." By this Solomon knew that the first lady was his real mother. She would not want him dead, no matter what. The king showed wisdom in action; his fame grew because of his wise actions. In the same way people will begin to realize that you have your "mental act" together, after you put your mind and heart to it.

Area 2: Physical—*But I'm No Hulk!*

You not only have a mental aspect; you have a physical side, too. Oh, you've noticed! Now that we have talked about your brain, how about your bod? Are you overweight? Try this: Eat less, work out more. Are you eating at least some good foods? (By the way, grease doesn't count.) Do you sleep away or TV away your weekends?

Don't feel bad. I know what it's like to be out of shape. As a teen I got my only exercise when I filled the tub, took a bath, pulled the plug, and fought the current. You wouldn't want to see a skinny kid sucked down the drain, would you?

I have many opportunities to visit and spend time in old folks' homes. Such visits helped me realize the importance of health. Without your health, you can do very little. Oh, many disabled people do great things, but it's truly sad to watch people in America overeat, overdrink, often stuffing themselves like Thanksgiving turkeys and then retiring to the sofa to spend five to six hours before the infamous boob tube. They watch other people make a good living while they get sore backs and become physically unfit.

Realize this. Being ordinary and going along with the crowd takes no effort at all. No one will ever applaud you. You'll never feel as good about yourself as if you had worked hard and reached for your star and found it. I only go round and round like this because I want the best for you. Don't miss out on the mountaintop experiences in life just because you've never tried.

Area 3: Spiritual—*He Grew in Favor With God*

Guess what? Along with having a mental and a physical side, you have a spiritual one as well. It's one of the legs on the chair on which you build your life—your future. If you break a leg on your kitchen chair, what happens? As long as you just look at it, it stands, but when you sit down and lean back, watch out. Chairs can't stand with two or three legs; they need four. Some chairs are designed to work with three legs. It's as though they gave up on the fourth leg and moved the three others around to form a triangle. Oh, it stays up as you sit on it, but it will never be one of the strongest chairs. A little leaning, and over you go.

What Does It Mean to Grow in Favor With God? I'm about to share my most important message with you, so please pay attention: I'VE NEVER KNOWN A TRULY HAPPY PERSON WHO WAS SUCCESSFUL AND AT PEACE WITH HIMSELF WHO DIDN'T HAVE A PERSONAL RELATIONSHIP WITH GOD. Mark 8:36 says, "For what shall it profit a person, if he shall gain the whole world, and lose his own soul?" *Everyone* needs God's favor.

How do you grow in favor with God? Just the way you would with anyone else. You get to know Him and spend time with Him. You talk to Him (we call it prayer) and let Him talk to you. He talks to us when we read His book or listen to people who know Him personally.

I got to know more about the importance of God in my life when I met Terry Bradshaw of the Pittsburgh Steelers. He spoke at a big rally in which I acted as a promoter. After his talk, long lines of people waited to shake his hand and have him autograph his book. He said to me, "Before I sign any books, you and I are going backstage to get down on our knees and thank God for making all this possible." We went backstage and prayed for about five minutes. Here he was, a Superbowl champion, yet he knew the importance of keeping that spiritual part of his life strong and intact.

For every example of a person walking with God, I can also give you ten examples of those who don't. Many, on the outside, seem happy and successful. Please understand this. If having money and fame is success (and that's the message from Hollywood), it still is not peace of mind. Even with all the world can give, you'll worry about who you are going to step on in the episode of "Dallas" or "Flamingo Road." If success means singing on stage and selling millions of records and becoming so famous you take your own life, I don't want it. If success is getting on TV and selling harmful items, I can't get excited about it. I don't need the money that badly.

Happy Outside, Sad Inside. I know what it's like to seem fine outside but feel miserable inside. All through my school years I looked down on myself in many ways. On the outside I seemed okay, because I was usually cracking a joke or trying to get someone's attention. I always looked at and wanted what I didn't have. I never appreciated or realized what lay right at my fingertips. I wanted to hang around with the popular kids. I didn't like my family. I never let my younger brother, Dale, play in any reindeer games. In fact, if I could embarrass him in front of others, I felt big and powerful.

I never applied myself in school. Getting mostly C's was good enough for me. College turned into one all-night cram session after another, and I barely stayed in school. Once I let a friend take a test for me, and we both got kicked out of the class.

Even the way I met my wife, Holly, showed my need for an honest foundation in my life. I first saw her in one of my classes in my junior college. A fellow next to me told me her name and what school she attended. I had moved there in the eleventh grade. I didn't know many people, so I thought we just never met. I went up to her and said, "You're Holly Hine, aren't you?" She said, "Yeah, but who are you?" I said, "Don't you remember me? I'm Bill Sanders. We went to Portage High School together." She said, "That's funny. I left in the eighth grade!"

Although my parents brought me up in the church, I never knew that you could know for sure if you were going to heaven or that you could talk directly to God. I didn't know that He would help me with everyday needs and fears.

Church was a joke to me. I would still lie and steal, if it benefited me. After I married Holly, I still lived like all the rest of my friends for three years. It seemed I was always at a bar or drinking. Since everyone else "ran around," I didn't think anything of it—besides, it made me feel important, and it built up my ego.

Holly found out I was unfaithful, and it just about killed her. It tore her heart apart. She left for a short while, and for the first time in my life I saw my whole world about to crash to the ground. For the first time I also knew how fortunate I was to have her and realized so many other things that I had always taken for granted.

If you were to drop a rubber ball, it would have to drop all the way to the floor before it would bounce back. Fortunately I didn't have to hit rock bottom before I realized my need for God.

I read a book by a great friend whom I deeply admire: *Confessions of a Happy Christian*, by Zig Ziglar. I felt God Himself speaking to me as Zig told how miserable his life was before he turned it over to God. Something started happening inside me. I felt an emptiness as never before. I've been told since that the heart is the exact shape of Jesus, and only He can fill it completely. I had tried popularity, and that didn't fill it. Neither did money, having my own way, being a "big shot," running my own company, or graduating from college. But I still didn't ask God to be a part of my life until I saw real courage in action.

My sister Nancy had just accepted Christ into her life a couple of months earlier. She and her husband had to hit rock bottom before they saw their spiritual depravity. Their third child, David, was born with an open spine. Operation after operation left them helpless, so they turned their fears and worries and David over to God. Everything about them changed. They became alive! They could handle their problems more easily, and they felt so excited about having met Jesus for the first time in a personal way. They had to share their wonderful news. Nancy came from Tennessee to Michigan to share with my entire family.

Believe it or not, we got angry at her for telling us she had something we didn't. A few weeks later her words hit me again as I realized her great love for us. Enough love to have her entire family walk out on her and call her a crazy fanatic. If she haa just found a cure for cancer and we all had it, she asked, wouldn't it be sad if she kept it to herself in Tennessee? Well, she found something more marvelous than a cure for cancer: It was a cure for eternity in hell.

By the way, do you know how long eternity is? A friend of mine received this definition from one of his young Sunday-school students. Eternity is this long: If you had a steel ball bearing the size of the world—solid steel—and you had an ant walk around and around it with endless energy, when the ball bearing had completely been worn away by the friction from the ant, eternity would have just begun.

Well, since I had the choice of where to spend eternity and with whom to spend the rest of my life here on earth, I chose Christ. On Christmas Day, 1978, I got down on my knees and said this simple prayer: "Dear God. I know I am a sinner, and I don't deserve anything but hell, but your Holy Word says that without Jesus in my life I will die in my sins. I'm so very sorry for all the wrong I have done and how I have hurt you and others. Please, dear Jesus, come into my life and be my Lord and Savior. Amen."

Jesus has lived in my heart ever since. Sometimes when I get wrapped up with myself or my business, He gets pushed aside, but He never leaves me. It's His promise. Life hasn't been perfect or easy. I still have my tough times and weak moments. If I can stay close to Him by reading His Word and hanging around others who know Him in a personal way, I can stay strong and uplifted.

Growing With God. A year or so after I became a Christian, I saw Zig Ziglar in action. Since he had been so important in my finding God, I held him high on my list of heroes. We were backstage at a speech Zig was to give in Las Vegas. I praised him and told how he helped change my life and how grateful I was to him. Wisely he saw that I had almost made him my idol. He said, "Let me share something with you, Bill. Don't ever look up to any man or woman the way you are to me. We will all falter and stumble. I've done things in my past that I'm

66

very ashamed of. Only look up to Christ that way. Put Him up there to be your model. He will *never* fail you."

Wow, I learned a great lesson that day. He could have basked in the glory of that moment, but instead he showed why he has such peace within himself. He gave the glory to God.

ACCEPTING JESUS AS YOUR PERSONAL SAVIOR IS THE MOST IMPORTANT THING YOU WILL EVER DO. The only thing more sad than to live your life without Christ, is to die without Him! God made us with freedom of choice at birth. We get to choose to live for Him or anything else. We can make Him our God, or we can make money, popularity, or material things our god. I know a man who made money and football his God. He owns a team. He has millions, his own jet plane. But one of his daughters has committed suicide en route to his so-called success. I wonder if money ever covers up the pain. For me it couldn't.

Well, now you know my story, straight from my heart. It's all for real. Even if you feel mad at me, think I'm forcing my faith on you, and reject everything I've said, I'll still love you with all my heart. I'll keep on praying that this book will be one of the steps to help you come to Christ. You see, I don't want to get the following letter from you some day:

> Dear Bill: It was great hearing you speak and reading your book. You made me laugh and told me how to live with myself and become my own best friend. You even showed me how to set and reach my goals, but why didn't you ever tell me that I needed Jesus in my life? You know how He helped your life. How come I am down here in hell? Why didn't you at least give examples of other people who turned their lives over to God? I might have done the same. I hold you accountable for my misery in eternity. Many people here were told to choose Christ, and they didn't, but I never even knew how important it was. You could have been the one, but you weren't. I can't call you friend. A

real friend would certainly have cared where I
spend forever and ever.

Sincerely,
Me

Area 4: Social—*But I'm Not a Loudmouth*

Becoming a Suzy Socialite or an Eddy Everything for everyone isn't a requirement for social success, but you do need to
develop skills in getting along with others. You are a social
creature. Maybe you enjoy being alone—that's okay. Just be
flexible and tolerate people and try to get along.

Studies show that people who get along with others receive
better pay in all kinds of professions. That doesn't mean you
need a real outgoing personality or must seem popular to get
along socially. Just be polite and listen to others. Encourage
them to talk, and become genuinely interested in what they are
saying. Never talk behind anyone's back, and only say positive
things about others when you do talk about them.

Once you take the first step toward becoming friends with
others, it will get easier and easier. By improving your social
standing, you will be closer to being a well-rounded person,
with your foundations built on the right principles.

What If I Don't? Almost every time I speak before an audi-
ence made up of teenagers, someone comes up to me after my
talk, telling how he has placed his entire life on one leg of his
foundational chair. Many tell how drugs or alcohol has literally
wrecked their lives. They wanted to be popular (social), so they
would do anything (drink, smoke, do drugs, sex) to get in and
stay in with the crowd.

Some girls tell how they have had to get abortions, or how
they have been having sex since they were thirteen or fourteen.
Their entire acceptance is wrapped up in the fact that someone
finds their bodies (physical) attractive.

Then there's the jock who is very popular (social) and great
at his or her sport (physical), but he or she can't cope after
graduation. (No spiritual or mental.) The world becomes too
rough a place. Such people thought everyone would treat them

FROM THE BOTTOM UP

as if they were the heroes of the home team. I wish they would wake up!

The beauty queen often doesn't stay married, because life isn't one prom after another. It's tough and it takes character and commitment. The same happens if you get lopsided in the mental area by always reading and improving your mind. Who wants to go out on a Friday night and study encyclopedias?

A person can also be overexcited about his spiritual side. If you drive everyone away and never talk about anything but the Bible, you will become a very lonely person. God doesn't want us to stay locked in the church all day, every day, reading the Bible. He wants us to be well-rounded, with strong, secure footholds on the social stone, physical stone, spiritual stone, and the mental stone.

Remember: Any strong area, overused, becomes your greatest weakness. For example, if you are a good talker and you talk, talk, talk, no one will be around for long.

But My Life Isn't Balanced!

Anyone who doesn't have a balanced life has some pain in his or her life. No one avoids every problem, but each of us can learn to deal with ours more successfully.

Two Ways Out

It's up to you how you chose to deal with your problems. As far as I can tell, you have two choices. Either you can cop out on your problems, hide from them, pretending they aren't there, or you can begin to deal with your troubles and end up with a deeper, richer life.

What About Suicide? So many teens have looked to death as a way out that suicide has become the second biggest killer among teenagers. What really causes a person to take such a drastic step? I believe it is the lack of a well-rounded life. Without a solid foundation, no wonder one can't stand.

A young man was state president of his youth organization. As a senior in high school he had everything going for him. One day his girl friend broke up with him. He thought his life was over, not worth living, so he killed himself! I would guess he placed way too much emphasis on the social area and not enough on the spiritual. If God walks with you, helping you each day, you can handle these normal, everyday negatives.

Many young people feel too frustrated with pressures from all sides to cope with life. No one seems to listen—no one seems to care. They have hinted for months to their families and best friends, but everyone seems too busy. The only way to get their attention is to commit suicide.

Remember this: Suicide is no way to handle your problems. It is a total cop-out, giving grief to everyone and helping absolutely no one. Suicide is Satan's ultimate victory over a person. Don't let him win.

If you are hurting so much right now that you want to take your own life, talk with someone who *will* listen. Call someone and tell him or her how you feel. Get it out in the open. I once felt like killing myself. A very special friend of mine thought I lied to him, and he completely disowned me! I went to him three or four times, and he acted as if I never existed. It ripped my heart apart so badly that I thought of nothing else except ending it all. I knew someone who would listen: my sister Mary. She's always been a special angel in our family. (God wasn't my best friend at the time, so I never thought of going to Him.) Mary just listened. She didn't give me any advice. She simply encouraged me to keep talking about it. She said to go ahead and cry. I did. It helped clean me out. The hurt wasn't completely gone, but I made it through. Then she helped me look at the situation realistically. He wasn't worth it. He just wasn't worth it.

Please find someone to talk to: a friend, a parent, a counselor or special teacher at school, a coach, your pastor, a neighbor— anyone who will sit and listen and hurt with you awhile! Please find someone now. Write to me at the address I've given at the end of the book, and I'll write back and pray for you.

But What Else Do I Do When It Hurts? What's the other choice? Starting to deal with your problems. List up to three things you have trouble with. Is it the mental side of your life? Do you have trouble with your studies? Thank God that He has given you a mind that works well (even if it doesn't get you straight A's). Lots of people don't even have that.

Does the physical give you trouble? Maybe you'd like to cut gym class permanently, because you do so badly. Or you have the longest nose in creation. Maybe you're so short you hit a basketball player's kneecap with your forehead, when you stand up straight. Big ears? Thank God that what you have works right: "Thanks, God, for these Spock ears. I sure can hear a lot." (Up to four blocks away.)

Maybe you don't even have a spiritual life. Thank God that He is interested in your life and wants to be a part of it. Ask Him into your life. Or maybe you've known Him for a long time, but have just ignored Him. Thank Him that He still hasn't given up on you. Start walking His way again.

Your social life might be so dull it makes walking the dog look exciting. Thank Him that you *can* have a social life, that there are people you can meet and those who already care about you.

Next, ask God to help you accept whatever your problem is. For instance, you can't lose weight. No matter how you try, you just can't seem to get thin. Once you take the blame off God and accept yourself, you will be better equipped to deal with it. The biggest single reason people who lose weight gain it right back is that they don't lose the weight in their minds. They still see themselves as fat. Put God on your side, and you will have the Creator helping you. Also, remember it isn't God who eats "one more bite."

Once you've accepted your accountability for the problem, focus on someone worse off. Visit a retirement home. You will realize how fortunate you are with your height or weight or looks. You can walk and run and set goals and dreams. Many of the people you will see there can't. Or you can go to the emergency room at the hospital some Saturday night. Watch as life-and-death situations come like snowflakes. You will realize how minor your negative features really are.

Others Have Made It!

No matter what your situation, there is hope. No matter how you feel about yourself, don't give up. No matter what you envision for your future, it can become better than that. No matter what people say to you or what they have said to you in the past, you can have a life full of happiness. You can have a life where you can live with yourself—and I don't mean when you turn thirty years old. Start that life *today*, but first believe you can do it. You have to believe what you are reading. I'm not feeding you mere words. Even now as you read this, I hope you will feel the way I feel as I am writing it. This book is in your hands so you will believe and act on it. The principles it describes can change your life. When I put some very simple priorities right in my life, my life changed. By putting God first, I could begin to believe in me, because I realized that I was created in His image. No longer would I see myself as a mistake with a missing link that can't explain where it came from. I'm not just someone who happens to be here. By the way, anytime someone tells you he believes in evolution, you just tell him this: "Evolution is the same as if a bunch of springs and a piece of glass and a band and a second hand and a minute hand and hundreds of little pieces were floating in space and through eternity, and because they evolved, they came together as a finely tuned, beautifully running watch." It is absurd.

My dad said it best. "Anyone who can't believe there is something greater than himself isn't very sharp." By the way, my dad graduated from the fifth grade, but in the game of life he has graduated cum laude (with honors). If Bill Sanders, who couldn't lead a group in silent prayer, could end up public speaking for a living, you, too, can find your song and sing it. Maybe you need more proof.

Having Hard Times? One businessman, whenever someone comes into his office bemoaning his misfortunes in business, love, or life in general, takes him aside and invites him to study a framed, hand-lettered sign hanging on the wall. It reads:

72

Failed in business—'31
Defeated for legislature—'32
Failed in business again—'33
Elected to legislature—'34
Sweetheart died—'35
Defeated for Congress—'48
Defeated for Senate—'55
Defeated for vice-president—'56

Suffered nervous breakdown—'36
Defeated for speaker—'38
Defeated for elector—'40
Defeated for Congress—'43
Elected to Congress—'46
Defeated for senate—'58
Elected president of the United States—'60

The name beneath this record of misfortune crowned by final success? *Abraham Lincoln.*

Here are some other people (some of whom you have not heard of and some you may have), but maybe you don't know what they have gone through. Maybe some of your heroes have had to go through things worse than you. In saying this, I am not trying to minimize your situation or your trials and pain, but I do want you to know that you can overcome them. Many other people have before you.

If you are crippled, you can still turn out to be a Sir Walter Scott.

Lock a man in a prison cell, and you have a John Bunyan.

Bury him in the snows of Valley Forge, and you have a George Washington.

Afflict him with asthma as a child, and you have a Theodore Roosevelt.

Put him in a grease pit of a locomotive roundhouse, and you have a Walter P. Chrysler.

Make him second fiddle in an obscure South American orchestra, and you have a Toscanini.

Spit on him, humiliate him, crucify him, and He forgives you, and you have Jesus Christ.

Strike him down with infantile paralysis, and he becomes FDR . . . Franklin Delano Roosevelt.

Drag him, more dead than alive, out of a rice paddy in Vietnam, and you have a Rocky Bleier.

Have him or her born black in a society filled with

racial discrimination, and you have a Booker T. Washington, Harriet Tubman, Marian Anderson, George Washington Carver, or Martin Luther King, Jr.

Make him the first child to survive in a poor Italian family of eighteen children, and you have an Enrico Caruso.

Call a slow learner "retarded" and write him off as ineducable, and you have an Albert Einstein.

Tell him he's "too stupid to learn," and kick him out of school at the third grade, and you have a Thomas Edison.

Tell her she's too old to start painting at eighty, and you have a Grandma Moses.

Afflict him with periods of depression so severe that he cuts off his own ear, and you have a Vincent van Gogh.

Blind him at age forty-four, and you have a John Milton, who, fifteen years later, had his masterpiece "Paradise Lost" published.

Call him dull and hopeless and flunk him in sixth grade, and you have a Winston Churchill.

Punish her with poverty and prejudice, and she may survive to become another Golda Meir.

Tell a young boy who loves to sketch and draw that he has no talent, and you have a Walt Disney.

Rate him as mediocre in chemistry, and you have a Louis Pasteur.

Amputate the cancer-ridden leg of a handsome young Canadian, and you have a Terry Fox, who vowed to run on one leg across the whole of Canada to raise $1 million for cancer research.

I'd also like to share some common stories I hear most every day from young adults who have decided to put effort forth and work on becoming a person who rolls over problems because he or she's well rounded. Remember the six areas outlined in chapter three.

"Since I've been talking at the dinner table [becoming more sociable], things seem to be going better for me in all areas of my life. It's even easier to go to church with my family. I'm working on my little sister now."

"Now that I've stopped worrying about my weight problem [physical], I am getting better grades, and my friends say I am easier to get along with."

"I've been looking at my blessed list and success list that we worked on, and you know what? It makes it easier for me to deal with my problems. I'm not nearly as depressed [mental] as I used to be."

"I've decided to start choosing the right friends [social]. You're right, it's not worth it to be around people who only want what you can do for them. It's hard to say no, but I'm already developing pride in myself. My living for God is the key. I realize God died for me. If He loved me that much, I'm not going to let Him down [spiritual and mental]."

"After your talk, I realized how much my parents love me. I made them feel awful because I used to hate to be seen with them. I'm a lot more grateful than ever before [family and mental]."

"I was one of those who thought making the team [physical and social] would answer all my problems. I'm going to work on the areas I can become good at. My goal is to make my 'mark' by becoming a veterinarian."

"I never realized how much my anger [mental] was controlling me. You are right. It's my choice. No one makes me angry."

"I've found Jesus! [spiritual]. Praise the Lord. It seems that I feel better about being here [physical and mental] and school doesn't get me down anymore [mental]."

"After today, I'm never again going to make fun of anyone [social]. Like you said, if I don't stand for something, I will fall for anything. Besides, I think I'll become one of the leaders of this school."

"I've thought about what you said about building my life on sand or rock. I'm going to church now [spiritual], and I'm exercising every night before bed [physical]. I already get along with others pretty well [social], and I get good grades [mental]. Now I'm striving toward my goal of being happy on the inside as well as the outside. Thanks for touching my life."

"I've been depressed for over a year now [mental]. No one knew I was drinking every day, not even my brother, and he shares my room [physical]. But, I've completely stopped! I'm not going to ruin my life. I'm going to AA. I'm going to tell my parents next week. Pray for me. They taught me to look to God for the strength I need. I can do all things through Christ who strengthens me."

I could go on and on and on. The books are filled with others who have overcome what you are going through right now. Become one of those fortunate few (and I do mean *few*) who build their lives on the right foundation, who apply the right principles to their life. Become happy. Life should be exciting. Sure you'll have sad times and sincere times and serious times, but you should live life in a way that you can live with yourself. I know you can do it. I wouldn't be putting so much of my life into this book if I didn't have faith in you. Please don't go along with what others say and do just to go along with the crowd. You have got a song in you, sing it!

Check Out Your Turf

1. How deep do your roots go? What kind of foundation are you built on? Write out a short statement (maybe a paragraph) about what you have as your foundation.
2. How does your foundation reflect wisdom? physical strengths? favor with God? favor with man? List your good points first and then look at areas for improvement.
3. Read a book or article on a real-life person who has overcome obstacles. Did the story inspire you? How did this person do it successfully? What can you learn from his or her story?

Part 2
OTHERS' TURF

- 5 -

THE PEER-PRESSURE JOURNEY

Let's take an exciting journey down the peer-pressure path. Every person who has ever lived has traveled on it. Some effortlessly fly down the road. Others get stuck or run off it. Some spin their tires and never go anywhere. Still others, affected adversely, have head-on collisions with invisible objects. Although such barriers seem invisible to onlookers, not so to the one who sees them in his mind. Thoughts like *I'm afraid! People might laugh, What will they think? No one cares about me, I'm not good enough,* and *I'll never make it* can end your journey. So much of peer pressure is really only mind games.

You might also be surprised to know that most peer pressure (or what people call peer pressure) does not come from peers at all. But there are ways in which *everyone* feels he or she needs to conform to what others think. Right now let's just mention a few:

The *media* apply pressure. They challenge and en-courage us to live, dress, and act like the superstars we see so often.

The *times we live in* tell us what to do, too. We may feel that we should live with someone before marriage. Everyone else does.

Parent pressure says: "Be a doctor like your grand-pappy," "You better get all A's. I did when I was your age," or, "The way you act, you are going to end up in jail."

Teacher pressure goes like this: "Can't you do bet-ter than that?" or the teacher rolls his eyes toward the ceiling when you ask a question he thinks is dumb.

Economic pressure hits today's teenager especially hard: "I must have a house this big," "a car this ex-pensive," "a bank account worth this much," "a job this prestigious," and, "clothes that look like his or hers."

Of course, you also face good old real peer pressure from your friends. Pressure to do something, be something, or go somewhere you don't want to. Don't forget, it *is* pressure! When you feel pressured, you feel you must act. You must do something! You can say yes or no. Stand there or walk away. Worry about it, or kill yourself over it. You might not let it bother you, or you might talk to someone about it, deal with it effectively. You can even share with others who have been through it before. For every problem we have, a hundred pos-sible solutions exist. Some are good and some are not. Some will destroy you, and some will make you even stronger when the next pressure comes along. A look at what we'll call "Others' Turf" will help you identify pressures and discover ways in which to deal with them.

As we look at others' turf, please remember no two people see anything exactly the same way. Because of our past experi-ences, our life-styles, the way we look at things, and the way we are used to having things happen to us, we just see things differently.

As I share some common problems and solutions, please look for meaningful ideas that can help you. For instance, if I say that peer pressure causes people to lie and lying will only hurt you and others, please give my conclusion a try, even if you now perceive lying to be okay.

I'm not asking you to believe everything I say. As far as that goes, you should not believe everything anyone says. But at least give these ideas a good chance and think about them so you can truly decide for yourself. That is also a good way to handle peer pressure. Think ahead of time what you are getting into before you blindly go running in.

Identifying Peer-Pressure Problems

Let's take the peer-pressure quiz to see if you suffer from today's number-one teen disease: peer pressuritis. After you take the quiz, you'll discover the most common types of pressures faced by young adults, and then we will look at specific strategies to overcome and effectively handle these pressures. The quiz, along with the material from the rest of these chapters, come from my interviewing and researching the problems of thousands of young people across America over the past five years.

Peer-Pressure Quiz

There are no right or wrong answers. I merely want you to identify where you are now so you can see clearly where you want to go in the future.

1. Do you wear the clothes you wear because you think others will approve?
2. Do you keep from wearing clothing that you know is different from the trends or something that will surely get others' attention?
3. Is your hairstyle in?
4. If your hairstylist wanted to experiment on you, would you say no?
5. If it were fifties day at your school, would you be too embarrassed to slick your hair back or wear a ponytail and white socks?

6. Have you ever held back from trying to get top grades because the people you hang around with wouldn't be comfortable?
7. Have you ever joined in with others as they were "putting down" or laughing at another student?
8. Would it be difficult for you to stop a fight or tell others not to pick on a certain student?
9. Even if you wear your seatbelt when you ride in a car, do you ever hold back from asking others to wear theirs?
10. Do you keep from wearing your seatbelt when someone else drives?
11. Do you feel a strong need to go to college or get into a certain profession because "significant others" expect you to?
12. Is it hard for you to go to your parents and discuss how you disagree with their expectations of you?
13. Do you avoid showing affection to a family member while around other students?
14. Do you avoid saying, "I love you," to a family member or a close friend?
15. If you wore braces, would it be hard for you to smile?
16. Do you feel embarrassed if others snicker at one of your questions in class?
17. Is it hard for you to ask disruptive students to be quiet during class?
18. Do you go to parties at which you feel uncomfortable?

19. At parties do you ever do things you don't believe in?
20. Do you watch or listen to TV programs, movies, and "in" music even though you don't agree with them?
21. Would it be hard for you to walk out of a movie if you were offended, even if you were with a group of friends?
22. Do you avoid sitting in a different place with different students in the cafeteria?
23. Have you ever wanted to go out for a sport or the school play but didn't?
24. Do you steal things or cheat on tests because a friend does?
25. Do you lie because your friends expect you to?
26. Is it hard to go to your parents with your problems and concerns?
27. Have you ever had a great idea but felt ashamed to tell anyone or share it in class?
28. Do you often disagree with your teacher but never say anything?
29. Have you ever felt like complimenting your teacher but didn't?
30. Is it hard for you to arrive earlier and stay later and work harder than other employees where you work?
31. Do you avoid praying before meals when you are out with friends?
32. Are you ashamed to share your religious convictions with other people, even if they ask?
33. Would it be hard for you to stay after practice (for any

sport) and work out, even if others scoffed at you?

34. Is it difficult for you to tell a friend, "I'm going to stay home tonight and work on my term paper"?

35. If you knew someone was ruining his life with drugs, would it be a tough decision for you to get the help he needs?

36. Would it be tough for you to go to a party and drink a Dr. Pepper if you knew everyone was drinking booze and would make fun of you?

37. If several students were leaving a party totally blitzed, would it be embarrassing for you to convince them not to drive but to ride with you?

38. If a fellow student had a real emptiness in her heart and felt she had nothing to live for, would you find it difficult to tell her about God or get her in touch with a counselor?

39. If you saw your boss stealing from the company you work for, would you confront him or her?

40. Is it almost impossible for you to invite a younger brother or sister to do something with you where you will be seen by your peers?

How to Score Your Quiz. Add up the total number of yeses.

If the total is above 25, you are deeply affected by peer pressure. You should work hard on raising your self-esteem and study the strategies provided in this book. Here are the sentences that best describe you: "You aren't who you think you are. You aren't even who others think you are, but you are who you think others think you are." You are greatly influenced by others' opinions of you— much more than your own opinions of yourself.

That does not mean you've come to the end of the world. It is never that bad. Even when you think you will never get over something in your life, remember: *YOU CAN!* If I had taken this little quiz at any time in my life before the age of twenty-three, I would have answered yes to about 35. That's right! 35. I spent my entire life seeking others' approval. What a loss of time! I wasted much of my life learning that lesson. Now I'm me! Applying the principles we talked about in the self-esteem chapters, I have built my life on the right foundations (mental, social, spiritual, and physical). I realize my worth as a person. Guess what? *If I can do it, so can you!*

If you scored between 10 and 25, peer pressure also affects you, but not as badly. You should be proud of the fact that you possess the self-confidence you have to say no to 15 to 30 of those questions. You are well on your way to becoming a person who can look in the mirror and always see his or her best friend. Now look over those questions you answered with a yes and analyze why you went along with public opinion.

If you checked between 0 and 10, you have others in your life who believe in you. Probably you have a great deal of self-confidence. Most likely you also can act very stubbornly, but the crowd doesn't have a choke hold on you as it does on 95 percent of today's youth and adults. At this stage I would advise you to work on your gentleness and concern for others. You may have become such an "individual" that you don't notice others. Think about it.

Let's Get Into It!

This isn't freshman peer pressure, class 101. You don't have to study terms and textbooks to know what this thing called peer pressure is all about. You do need to be in control of it and not have it in control of you.

I'll outline our peer-pressure journey, which will last for three chapters. Come back to this overview when you need to identify what type of pressure is getting at you, as well as the source and the reason for it.

Types of Pressures You Face
1. Helpful (when conforming to these pressures, we better ourselves)
2. Harmful (when conforming to these pressures, we hurt ourselves)
3. Ho hum (when conforming to these, we stay neutral—neither helped nor harmed)

Two Primary Sources Send These Pressures
1. Others (other-inflicted pressures)
2. Ourselves (self-inflicted pressures)

The Greatest Reasons Why People
Give in to Pressures
1. Low self-esteem
2. Fears of all kinds
3. The need to be accepted
4. Don't know how to say "no"

Giving in to peer pressure causes us to behave according to the conduct of the group (their behavior style). Just as the force applied to a nail by a hammer alters it, peer pressure demands a result or a change in behavior. The nail can hold firm, or it can give in, but either way the nail experiences stress. It feels that direct blow from one end to the other. Like that nail, you feel pressure from the world around you. How does it influence you? First let's identify which pressures have a poisonous sting and which don't.

Helpful Pressures

Any positive pressures that encourage us to better ourselves and grow fall in this category. As when you are encouraged to:

1. Go out for the school play
2. Run for a class office
3. Try out for the team
4. Read a book
5. Get better grades
6. Lose weight and get in shape
7. Develop a better grade of friends
8. Stop drinking or taking drugs
9. Start attending church regularly and reading the Bible more
10. Develop good study habits
11. Get serious about your personal growth
12. Appreciate your family more
13 Communicate with your parents
14 Tell "trusted others" your problems

15. Help out in your community
16. Contact colleges or future places of employment
17. Save your money
18. Learn new words
19. Develop self-confidence when speaking to people

Notice: These helpful pressures can be encouraged by you or by others.

Most helpful pressures will be applied to you by people who love you and care for you. These folks have something invested in you.

1. Your parents, who have invested years of sacrifice, love, money, and commitment, keeping you fed, clothed, and sheltered
2. Your true friends, who have invested months or years of sharing the important things, experiencing life, arguing, growing up, and unselfishness
3. Others who fall into this helpful area include: other family members; spiritual leaders; teachers, principal, or counselor; coach, band or vocational teacher at school; your mentor or hero

You may think some of these people have applied harmful pressures to you. True. No one's perfect, and just as others have let you down in the past and will in the future, you will at times let yourself down, because at times you apply harmful pressures to yourself. Don't get heavy on the blame here. Instead become aware of how others influence you. With you lies the decision whether or not a person acts in your best interest. You decide whether or not to follow your teacher's advice, do as your coach tells you, or obey your parents. Each of us has freedom of choice, and we must use it effectively in our lives. Caring and concerned people will *help* you in difficult decisions, but *you* make the ultimate choice. (A word of caution: Don't keep from following the advice of an authority figure just because he or she seems to be a hypocrite. Look instead at the advice you receive. Is it good? If so, take it!)

How Does It Work? This kind of pressure can really work to change lives! I told you before about my experience with the Dale Carnegie course. The first four weeks I was scared out of my socks to get up and give my two little talks at each of the sessions (each talk only lasts one or two minutes). When the fifth session came along, I gave my speech on "something you are really excited or mad about." I told about how a roommate of mine kept jumping on my furniture and breaking or damaging everything in sight. The class enjoyed it so much they gave me a standing ovation.

The next week before session six, I made a decision. I decided to quit the course. My instructor, Don Davies, couldn't believe his ears when I told him. He told me I had a definite speaking talent and it would be a shame not to finish the course and continue to develop it. He tried and tried to convince me, but no use. I closed my ears. It was as though I didn't even hear him. I had completely shut off my mind. When my parents would give me advice or suggestions on how to drive or who they felt was good company for me to keep, I used to do the same thing. I disregarded their many years experience of knowing what people are like and seeing character flaws. (Parents are usually pretty good judges as to who will be positive or negative influences in their kids' lives. My mom could size up my new friends after just ten minutes. That's the reason I advise parents to meet and talk to the boy before they let their daughter go out on a date with him and never to let her go if he waits in his car and honks his horn.)

Don never gave up. He wrote me and called me several times until I took the course again the next year. (What convinced me was his total interest in me. He already had my money, so the time he spent on me was time that could have been spent selling additional enrollments. He showed integrity.) I think, more than anything, I took the course again just to get him off my back. This time, though, I showed him that he was believing in the right person, because I didn't quit until the seventh session. That's right. I felt frightened all over again. Each talk got a little easier, but they still seemed too hard to take. Guess what? He *still* bugged me to finish the class. He said, "I know you don't believe me when I tell you of your ability to get ideas across while speaking, but it's true. You've *got* to finish this. Get it behind you. Don't be a quitter. Come on, if you haven't got any faith in yourself, use mine. I've got enough for both of us."

I took the course the third time, finished it, lost most of my fear of speaking, and ended up working with Don for the next two years. During this time I decided to be a public speaker the rest of my life.

Don applied positive, helpful peer pressure for two years and, with his integrity to go along with it, I couldn't pass up that combination.

Look around and find people who are trying to help and encourage you to do something. If they are acting in your best interest (and most of them are), listen to them and let a wiser, more mature person influence your life as Don Davies did mine. You'll be superduper glad you did.

A *word of caution:* For every person truly interested in you and your future, there are 10,000 who aren't. Ask the key question "What do you have to gain if I follow your advice?" Many people trying to "sell" you things fall in this category. I bought my house from a real-estate salesman who never told me that the payments on the house would never pay it off. I totally took his word and advice that this was a good and fair deal. After three years of making every single monthly payment, I owed more than when I started. I've also had bad experiences with some (not all by any means) insurance salespeople. Now I'm smart enough to know that I must do my homework. You should, too. Look into people and their pasts. Find out their true motives for encouraging you.

Harmful Pressures

Pressures that lead to actions that harm us in one way or another might be fun for a while, but ultimately they do damage. Without my listing all of them, you know what I'm talking about. Every teen gets a chance to say no—or yes—to the wrong things. From drugs, to sex before marriage or joining a satanic cult, negative peer influences try to squeeze into our lives every moment.

When deciding on following a certain crowd, being part of a specific group, smoking, drinking, or shooting up this or that, remember that you are also choosing what to:

1. Act like
2. End up like
3. Be treated like by this group and by others

If you choose cigarettes, you choose to: lose over eight years of your life; cough; have bad breath, yellow teeth, and a greater chance of cancer.

If you decide to drop out of school you actually choose: a low-paying job; hard, long hours; ignorance in many areas; and the possibility of friends who can't get ahead either.

If you choose crime, you actually choose: disrespect; a possible prison term; a life of looking over your shoulder.

If you choose to have sex before marriage, you actually choose: to play by your rules, not God's; to possibly get pregnant; a good chance of lack of respect for the other party; a 75 percent chance of divorce, if you marry as a teen; and maybe even a life of living on welfare.

When you choose a life-style or habit, you actually choose the end result of that habit or life-style. It can work in either direction—positive or negative. Let's see how the right choices can help.

Recently I met a young man who was a bellman at a large hotel. As he picked me up from the airport, I noticed several significant things about him that made him very pleasant to be around and an excellent employee. First, he came five minutes early to pick me up. I appreciated that, and when I asked, "Have you been waiting long?" he replied, "Just five minutes, sir, but you're the customer, and you're worth it." Wow! What a great start. He said, "You wait here, and I'll get the limo." That's right: a giant, navy blue, Cadillac limousine. He came back in a flash, grabbed my bags, and opened my door.

As we drove, I asked him how his day was going. I usually receive anything but an enthusiastic answer when I ask this question during the 5:00 P.M. rush hour, but not this young man. He told me, "It's been a great day so far, and I'm going to work hard to keep it that way." I asked how long he'd been working for the hotel. "Three years, and I love the work," he answered. "I know I'll always have a job where I'll be dealing directly with people."

"What causes you to have such a pleasant outlook on life and such a good attitude?" I wondered aloud. Without a moment's hesitation, he said simply, "My family upbringing. We were brought up in a strong, Christian home with parents who loved us and always gave me advice." "Didn't you resent that?" "No, sir," my driver responded. "I've always figured if someone takes the time to offer me advice, I'll at least listen to him. I make up my own mind if that advice is for me before I act on it, but I do listen. I'm glad people tell me things like that."

By this time each of us felt very comfortable talking with the other. He shared how he was able to stay away from drugs because he looked on them as bad advice. Before acting on it, he always looked over the advice of others. Was it good for him? Was it the right thing to do?

The young man carried my bags to my room, turned on the TV, adjusted the temperature, showed me where the lights were, explained how room service works, and asked if he could get me any ice. What a pro! I gave him a big tip and asked him to come down to the main ballroom the next evening at eight o'clock. I shared this brief story with 1,400 future business leaders at a large state convention and introduced him to the group, which gave him a standing ovation. Then I wrote a personal note to the president of the his corporation.

Isn't it something that today in America, when someone gets treated properly with respect and a pleasant attitude, it is the exception to the rule?

If you learn *now* to avoid the pressure to be mediocre and to act polite around people, showing a great attitude, you will never have trouble getting a job or being a success. When I asked this young man if he ever received job offers from other customers who appreciated his attitude, he said he gets about one a month. Realize that *you* are in charge of your life, and no one else will ever have to pay the price of your not doing your best or becoming what you know you could become. You've got greatness in you. Go out and show it to the world.

Ho-hum Pressures

These pressures don't make much difference as far as the end results are concerned. For example: If you walk the way your weird friend walks, it probably won't affect your grades or health. (Of course, that depends on how weird your friend really is!) Or if someone pressures you to sit in another seat in class, your grades or popularity won't really be affected.

Ho-hum pressures are so insignificant that you aren't influenced one way or the other. I mention them so you will know that some pressures are neutral. They just don't mean very much.

But do watch out if little, insignificant pressures start to grab you: You may be turning into a chameleon. Just recently I was at a speakers' convention (speakers and meeting planners go to this kind of meeting) for a couple of days. I noticed I had started dressing like everyone else: navy blue suit, white shirt, and burgundy tie. My hair had to be perfect, or I wouldn't leave the room. If the wind was blowing, I wouldn't look into it. I wanted to make sure a hair didn't leave its place. The last day there I noticed something strange: I had begun parting and combing my hair like everyone else. They all parted their hair on the side, and I had always parted my hair down the middle. That morning, before the meeting, I tried to get my hair to be something it wasn't. As soon as I realized what I was doing, I immediately wet my hair and put it back the way I enjoy wearing it. I also put on my blue shirt instead of a white one.

Please realize that I didn't wear old jeans and a cut-off sweatshirt. I would have been foolish and a bad business person if I had looked so different that none of the meeting planners would ever have hired me again. But I conformed within my own standards. You must do the same. Be yourself, but don't be so far out that the people you want to respect you can't because you are too foreign to them. It's called balance or a happy medium.

Check Out Your Turf

1. How have you felt peer pressure from the media? the times you live in? your parents? your teachers? economic problems? How have you handled them?
2. How does peer pressure influence you? If you haven't taken the peer-pressure quiz, do it now. Take a look at your answers. Where were your strong points? the weak ones?
3. List some of the helpful pressures you've experienced. How have you become better through them?
4. List some of the harmful pressures placed on you. How can you fight back?
5. List some of the ho-hum pressures in your life. Are any of them starting to become helpful? harmful?

-6-

TAKING THE *PRESSURE* OUT OF PEER PRESSURE

Peer pressure is really a misleading term in a way—it probably implies that others are trying to tell you what to do or setting the standards for the way you act, dress, and perform. But if you remember the outline I gave you in the last chapter, you'll know that I gave you two sources of peer pressure: others and ourselves.

Good news! Three out of four kinds of "peer" pressure fall into the second category—we cause it ourselves! Why is that good news? Because we can control our own thoughts and actions better than we can those of other people. You have hope!

Here are the four kinds of peer pressure:

"Follow the crowd" pressure
"Can't be me" pressure
"Afraid to try" pressure
"Me pressuring me" pressure

Let's see how they work.

"Follow the Crowd" Pressure

Others put this pressure on us by words, actions, or even just looks. "Follow the crowd" peer pressure makes us want to be just like everyone else—break dance when everyone else is break dancing, go to the movies all the other kids see, and become best friends with the most popular boy or girl in the class. Everyone seems to do it. So what's wrong with this attitude?

You've seen it. Four hundred sparrows will fly into the branches of a tree. (After all, that's what trees are for.) Then one daring, little brown sparrow will fly over to the chimney on the house. All of a sudden you hear a thunderous roar. When you look up you see 399 more sparrows flying—where? That's right: to the chimney. You yell up to the frantic flying flock, "Where are you going?" What do you think they say? "To the chimney, where else?" "Why?" "Because *he* did." You say, "Who's he?"

"Who knows? We are just following."

Of course, when they get there, they find that the chimney only holds fourteen sparrows, so most of them end up flying back to the tree. Your curiosity gets the best of you, so you ask the first sparrow why he flew to the chimney, and he tells you, "My widdle feet got code!"

People often act like those birds: One person has a reason for doing something, but the others just follow blindly along.

People and birds aren't the only ones. Sheep do the same thing. Let's say you have 100 sheep standing in line, waiting to jump over a gate. If you take down the gate in the middle of the line, the rest of the sheep keep jumping over the gate that is not there. They just jump because the one in front of them jumped. No other reason. They are all followers: They simply can't think for themselves.

In my assembly programs you should see the response I receive when I tell teens, "Raise your hand if you can think for yourself." Many students immediately raise a hand. However, many others wait until a friend or someone they think is cool raises his hand first. They must say to themselves, *You think for yourself.... Okay, so do I.* I have actually watched students put their hands down and others follow.

Some Following Is A-okay

There is nothing wrong with following the crowd—*if it is the right crowd!* Are you doing what you want to be doing and going where you want to be seen going? Today, you hear a lot about being a leader or a follower. Most great leaders *were* followers—followers of other great leaders. Such people sought out those with sound ideas and principles. They followed people who had a positive track record, a record of leading people to reach their top potential, feel good about themselves, and do right. The followers of Adolf Hitler, Jim Jones, and Charles Manson should have checked out the past records of these leaders before blindly becoming sparrows or sheep.

A friend of mine, a very successful business person, opens almost every talk he gives with a story about how the right kind of following made him a millionaire. That's absolutely right. In his mid-thirties he has success, wealth, and a beautiful family. He came from Lebanon to America in the mid-1960s and didn't know one word of English. Today, he is one of the top-paid professional speakers and consultants. His name is Nido Qubein. He's really got his act together, and it all started because of the right kind of peer pressure.

The most influential person in Nido's entire life? his mother. When he was a young boy, she told him, "Nido, if you want to be great, walk hand in hand with people who are great. If you want to be wise, walk hand in hand with people who are wise." So he worked hour after hour to learn English and now speaks with hardly a flaw. He walked with older and more experienced people. When they offered advice, he readily accepted it. He felt thankful for a tip on earning money or an idea for becoming popular with people and so on. What's in this for you? Simply this. Choose who you learn from and hang around and become like. You will most certainly become like your environment.

"Can't Be Me" Pressure

We usually cause our own "can't be me" peer pressure by wearing a mask to cover up our real selves. No one told us to wear one or said they didn't like us, but we wear the mask anyway. We build an invisible, thick, and almost unbreakable wall around ourselves.

"Can't be me" affects us when we constantly dream of being someone else. When I was in school, I wanted to be Elvis Presley. I thought if I could just sing like him I would be a success. By the way, if you ever heard me sing, you would be glad I took up speaking for a career. I even thought that if my name was *Elvis* I would have it made. Guess what? Happiness and success are not in your name, where you live, or how you look. It simply lies in who you are and what you do. Be yourself (who you really are) and believe in your actions or don't do them (what you do), and you won't always want to be someone else or follow the wrong crowd.

When someone tries to impress others by stretching the truth, he's fallen into the "can't be me" pressure trap. Such lying always comes back to haunt him.

When I was about ten years old I remember trying to be someone I was not. As I walked home from school, though it was forbidden, I wanted to hitchhike home. I kept walking, trying to get up the nerve to stick out my thumb. When I finally held my hand out, a car stopped. I didn't know what to do, so I got in. The problem was, I was in front of our next-door neighbor's house. The driver said, "How far are you going?" I didn't have the nerve to say forty feet, so I had him drop me off a mile down the road. I felt very embarrassed getting out in the middle of a cornfield and walking back.

"Afraid to Try" Peer Pressure

This type of pressure, also self-inflicted, keeps us from ever knowing our true potential. We feel "afraid to try" things for many reasons:

1. People might laugh
2. I might make a fool of myself
3. I might fail
4. I might succeed: Then everyone would expect me to do even better next time
5. I don't know how
6. I'm not worth it (low self-esteem)

So what if people laugh? They laughed at Thomas Edison, Mother Teresa, and Martin Luther King, Jr. People only laugh when they are afraid to try something themselves or when they feel insecure and putting someone down picks them up.

I'm not trying to oversimplify not letting others affect you. It hurts. I know it hurts. Doing most anything foreign to you feels scary. We all are afraid of something. Each of us has fears and vulnerable areas. Take the biggest, meanest bully in your school, and I can melt him down to putty in two seconds. Have him walk outside in the dark (most bullies are afraid of the dark) and walk straight into a spider's web—all over his face. He'll go nuts. Your bully will flinch, move faster than he has ever moved in his life, and claw at his face like you won't believe. When he gets done, tell him you think a big black spider just crawled in his left ear. You'll have him carrying your books for a year if you help him get through this life-threatening situation.

It works the same way when you won't try something because you might fail. So what? What's so bad about failing at things? Everyone is a failure at something. Jack Nicklaus fails at many things: heart surgery, electrical engineering, as a short-order cook! Because he doesn't do these things, you could call him a failure at them. But he does stick to his "thing": golf. He even fails at golf. If he plays eighteen holes of golf and scores a seventy, guess how many times he failed?

Fifty-two. If the goal of golf is to put the ball in the cup (and it is), then in eighteen holes, he missed the goal fifty-two times.

Terry Bradshaw has won more Superbowl games than any other quarterback in the game, yet he is one of the biggest failures at football as well. I would estimate that for every touchdown he made (success), he didn't make one on about fifteen other plays.

I enjoyed going to Alaska and speaking to a large delegation of high-school students in March, 1985. While I stayed there, one story made the news headlines every single day. No one wanted to miss telling about the dogsled race from Anchorage to Nome. For several weeks the dogs and the drivers faced blizzards, 40-degree-below-zero weather, and all kinds of elements. Because a caribou came out of the woods and attacked and killed several of his sled dogs one driver even had to quit the race.

On the front page ran the story of a female driver who led the race. She finally won! The first female to win in the history of the race. How did she do it? She wasn't afraid to try something that every other driver, by peer pressure, wouldn't do.

A blizzard ahead of one of the resting stopovers wouldn't let up. Everyone waited, except her. She went on following the trail, right through the middle of it. As it turned out, it got worse behind her and eased up a bit in front of her. The other mushers had to wait even longer. With a lead that no one could capture, she triumphantly won the race.

That woman took a risk—a very real chance. Not a stupid one, but a calculated one. She had trained hard. She was a pro. Unlike everyone else, she didn't sit and wait for a storm to get worse. After she thought about it, she got moving. That's for you as well. Go out and give this world and all its people your very best. Don't "go get 'em." Instead, "go give 'em" all your best.

I'm not implying you'll never fail. But don't let it stop you. We are all failures and winners at different things. At one point in his career, Babe Ruth held the record for the most home runs (successes) as well as the most strikeouts (failures). Lucille Ball was in her forties before she started the "I Love

Lucy" show. Winston Churchill would have died a miserable failure if he died before age seventy.

Let's stop *crying* and start *trying!* Let's stop *booing* and start *doing!*

"Me Pressuring Me" Pressure

Most of the pressures that affect us we apply to ourselves through our own self-talk. The classic example is the teen with braces. Because she thinks everyone will make fun of her, she tries never to open her mouth, smile, or eat in public. Even after the braces are off, she doesn't smile because of habit.

Guys do it when they ask a girl for a dance. Just by the way one walks and holds his head you can tell if he expects her to say yes or no. He's already talked himself into an answer. Most young men, when asking a girl out for a date, say to themselves, *She's probably busy. Besides, she doesn't like me anyway, and even if she said yes, it would be because she felt sorry for me.*

Who puts ourselves down most? We do! We talk to ourselves more negatively than any of our friends would dare to. Negative self-talk takes place when we play negative make-believe with words. Don't forget: Words are powerful. What you say to yourself gets etched on the microdisk in your brain. When you say things over and over (*I can't do it. I'm no good. Things never work out for me. I know I'll flunk. She'll never hire me*), the etching becomes deep, hard-to-remove grooves. Of course, positive self-talk influences you, too. You can smooth out old negative grooves and etches by applying positive statements over and over and over to erase them. Young people who grow up with child abusers as parents have a lot of positive smoothing out to do.

If your parents or the authority figures in your life have continually pumped in negative, damaging statements such as, "You're a loser," "You're stupid," "You'll end up in jail someday," "Can't you ever do anything right?" "Clumsy!" "Boy are you fat!" and so on, you'll have a lot of erasing to do, too. You must realize that parents don't all have positive self-images either. Many have never been exposed to these self-help ideas and specific ways to raise self-esteem. Become a positive influence in your parents' lives by lovingly sharing some of the techniques you've learned here.

Moving Ahead

Now that you can identify the sources of peer pressure in your life, you can begin to fight them. Chapter seven will give you fifteen ways to avoid peer pressure and make the most of yourself. Whether you are your own worst enemy or whether others seem to put most of the pressure on you, you can start to win the battle. You can be a success—it's up to you!

Check Out Your Turf

1. Why is the term *peer pressure* misleading? Who causes most peer pressure?
2. List the four kinds of peer pressure. Who causes each? Describe how each can work in your life. How have they influenced you? What can you do about it?
3. When is peer pressure okay? When is it all right to do what someone else does? When has this worked well in your life?
4. Share what you have learned about peer pressure with someone else. Tell him or her how knowing about it has helped you.

-7-

FIFTEEN WAYS TO AVOID HARMFUL PEER PRESSURE

If I had had this chapter to read and guide me while in high school and college, I'm positive I would have acted in a totally different way. I would have been myself. I would have dared to be different, try new things. Most of all, I would have shown the world the real Bill Sanders. Instead, it got a great big *phoney!* But not you. In this chapter you have strategies that will help you fight off peer pressure and free yourself from all the self-doubt and confusion that go along with it. As you read and study these strategies (ways to fight specific types of peer pressure) circle the ones that mean the most to you or cut them out and tape them to your bathroom mirror so you can learn what to say and how to act when you need to.

Strategy 1: Learn Positive Self-talk. Positive self-talk is very important. I meet thousands of people who have never even heard of it, let alone tried it or practiced it on a regular basis. For me, it has become my constant companion, wherever I go. On a way to a speech, I'm talking to myself in an optimistically expectant way. I imagine the best happening. I anticipate great outcomes in everything I do.

Use these rules for effective positive self-talk:

1. The sentences must be short and exact.
2. They must be positive.
3. They don't have to be true at this moment. (In most cases you will be telling the truth in advance, that's all.)
4. They must reflect what you want to come true.
5. Say them to yourself or out loud (in your car alone or in your room).

Try it on for size in a real-life situation.

SITUATION: You think you might be pressured to take drugs at a party you are going to attend Friday night. You are going because you want to meet some new people.

POSITIVE SELF-TALK: (You say this to yourself whenever you think of it, for about two days prior to the party.) *I have self-respect. I only put good things into my body. I enjoy being healthy. I have confidence. I stand up for what's right. People respect my decisions. I have lots of friends because I stand on my beliefs. That party will be a great time. I am a person of integrity. I believe in me and so do others.*

That's it. It will take about a minute to say all of those sentences to yourself. Write them on a card until you can come up with affirming statements whenever you need them. Notice all the sentences are positive. I didn't mention drugs, because your subconscious mind will concentrate on whatever you put into it. That is why you used words like: *integrity, respect, healthy, stand for right, great time,* and *beliefs.*

SITUATION: You are about to take a difficult test that you have studied hard for.

POSITIVE SELF-TALK: *I'll do great on this test. My mind is clear. I remember all the answers. My concentration is superb today. My studying always pays off. I'm well prepared. I love challenges. I'm going to have fun during this hour.*

At first your mind will go into shock at this new kind of programming. It's used to saying to you, *I know I'll flunk this test. I can never remember when the pressure is on. I hope I studied the right material.*

Great athletes and musicians have done this for years. They see the home run in their minds before they get up to bat, or they picture their instrument responding beautifully.

SITUATION: Everyday positive self-talk to help self-esteem.

POSITIVE SELF-TALK: *I am a good person. I make friends easily. I make the right choices. I know right from wrong. People admire me. I get good grades. I work hard. I'm a happy person. Great things always happen to me. I have a lot to live for.*

Strategy 2: Challenge the System! Don't take for granted that the only way to popularity is to go along with the crowd. Tell Hollywood to jump in a lake. Shout out to the people who are selling booze on TV. Tell them you know they want to make money and they don't give a hoot about people's lives, lost jobs, or wrecked homes.

The system says all beautiful people have it made. Is this true? Is this right? Is it just? If you don't believe so, do something about it. Don't let the system suck you down to its level. Rise above it. Get mad and do something about it.

If the filth during the movie offends you, walk out! Let people know you are a person of action, not a wimp who lets others run over him or her. Don't let others design success and happiness formulas. Challenge the system. It's your life.

Challenge the lyrics in your music. Question your parents if they drink and then say you can't use drugs. Don't disobey them, just question their drinking or their driving habits, and so on. You are a young adult. Decide for yourself.

Strategy 3: Get a Hero. Find someone whom you respect and admire. Remember: A good hero (someone to model our lives after) must be well rounded in all areas of life: social, spiritual, mental, and physical and treats *all* people with respect. To me a hero must be someone who is similar to you, sharing common interests. He has made it through the tough times and is at peace with himself. He has gained other people's respect because of that. He has many friends, because he becomes friends to many people. He challenges the system and says no to things he feels are wrong and doesn't believe in. He doesn't ever have to look over his shoulder and wonder what he did wrong. He is busy striving for his goals and desires.

Heroes are not perfect. No one is. Don't discard a hero because of one blemish in his or her character. Look for honesty. Look for someone who knows his God and himself, one who knows the power of prayer and the power of love.

Heroes can be alive or dead. You may have read about one. Don't make yours a "surface" hero. Look deeper, beyond the outer success, and find true character. Start looking. You'll find someone to look up to.

Strategy 4: Stop Living for Compliments. Because of their deep need for approval of others, teens often get involved with wrong groups or activities. Such outer-motivated people live for compliments, because their view of themselves comes from others and not from within themselves.

Compliments sound nice, but don't do things just to receive them. Sadly, most compliments aren't even sincere. They are only flattery. Webster defines *flattery* as, "insincere or excessive praise . . . a pleasing self-deception." Don't let others deceive you or live for the positive remarks others say about you. Live for a cause, a purpose—for God—and for your future.

Truly great people never work or strive for compliments or money or fame. They followed their hearts' desires and fulfilled the greatness inside them. The money, fame, and compliments often came in the end. That is what I want for you as well. Show the world the true, exciting, achieving you.

Strategy 5: Don't Build Relationships Just to Be Popular. Don't build relationships with people in the wrong group because you need popularity. Popularity with thieves is a terrible goal. The same with people who lie, do drugs, get drunk, cheat, and backstab others. If you must offend them, do it! Don't keep hanging around people with whom you disagree because you don't want to hurt their feelings. Get on with your life.

Strategy 6: Become a Thermostat Not a Thermometer. Most teenagers act like thermometers. They go along with everything around them. You can tell if they are 98.6 degrees (normal) or 110 degrees (burning up because of peer pressure). Thermometers have no control over their environment. They just reflect what goes on around them. Like chameleons, they change, depending on who they are with and what is happening.

The thermostat works differently. It is independent. It chooses the temperature. If it wants the room to be hot or cold or anywhere in between, it makes the final decision. In the same way, the thermostat-type young person decides what activities to go to and what results he or she wants in life.

One speaker told me a story about a girl who was almost totally rejected by her peers, but through sticking to her beliefs she gained a tremendous amount of self-respect. It seems, in her school, they weren't allowed to say the pledge of allegiance to the flag. But this girl believed in all that the flag stood for and started to fight for it.

She started getting signatures on her petition. Many of her friends told her she was wasting her time. Her boyfriend said he would stop dating her, if she didn't stop making such a big deal about it. It didn't matter to her. She kept on and finally got enough names on her list. Today in her Arizona school, they are saying the pledge of allegiance, because one girl stood up for her beliefs, even when others around her didn't.

When you take a stand and become a thermostat, you can help your hometown, school, or even hundreds of lives—like one girl who walks the streets of Los Angeles's Sunset Blvd. She doesn't look or act like a prostitute—because she isn't. Her name is Lois Lee. Her mission: giving homeless child prostitutes a choice. She has brought more than 250 youngsters to her apartment and given them friendship, hope, and a new beginning.

People told Lois she was crazy for doing this. They said, "You can't help these people. You're wasting your time." Her peer pressure didn't bother her. Today she has a Hollywood office with thirty volunteers and six paid employees. Her organization, "Children of the Night," offers counseling, free clothing, and a street outreach program. The world is better off with peer-pressure fighters such as Lois Lee.

You, as the thermostat, are in control of saying no to this or yes to that. No one turns you up or down. You do it yourself. You are the decision maker for your life and no one else. It's your choice. You could change the world because of it! Choose to be the thermostat—not the thermometer.

Strategy 7: Self-respect Versus Peer Reject. This strategy, as with the thermostat, is a matter of choice. Many times your decision to belong to a certain group and become involved in their activities will result in losing your self-respect. If you don't reject your boy- or girl friend's plea to have sex, you will lose your self-respect. If you don't "peer reject" those who do drugs, you end up being treated like them, and your self-respect goes down the tubes.

One girl was in college, and the pressure was all around her to smoke marijuana. Everyone did it, and it seemed harmless enough, as well as the "in" thing to do. She would go out on dates with her boyfriend and another couple, and everyone smoked dope but her. This girl made a decision to say no. Many times they all tried to encourage her, but she continually held her ground. Today she can look back with a great feeling about herself. She has even more strength to say no to other things as they come up. I'm very proud of her: You see, she's my wife, Holly.

You make the choice: self-respect or peer reject. Quite often you must say no to one in order to say yes to the other. If it comes down to a choice of your losing your self-respect or keeping it, choose to say no to the group and yes to yourself and your self-respect.

Remember this: If you lose your self-respect, no one can find it again but you. Once you lose it, it's hard to regain.

Strategy 8: Conflict Versus Conformity. Here's another choice. Conform or be different and face some conflict. You can't satisfy everyone, so decide for yourself who is on your side and who isn't. Conform to the helpful peer pressures and determine individually which cause harm. No one promised you an easy life. Conflict won't kill you. No one in history has died from it. The results of conflicts can cause you to make a stand, but that's what makes life interesting—standing on your convictions.

Very real conflict didn't stop Jill Kinmont. At eighteen, she was one of the most celebrated downhill skiers the United States had ever seen. *Sports Illustrated* put her on its cover. Her main goal in life was to earn an Olympic Gold Medal, but her entire world crashed to the ground in January, 1955. She had a skiing accident that left her paralyzed from her shoulders down.

After years of relearning to eat and read and write, Jill had a new burning desire inside of her. She wanted to be a teacher. She interviewed at UCLA, but they said she couldn't become a teacher. Teachers had to be able to stand before a class, and she was confined to a wheelchair. In 1963 she shared her goal of becoming a teacher with the College of Education at the

University of Washington. She studied hard and did well in school. She finally got her first student-teaching job. She loved kids and especially enjoyed working with students who were labeled "slow learners" or "hard to teach." She earned her teaching credentials, but when she was about to search for a full-time teaching job, tragedy struck. Her father died. She and her family moved back to California, where she wasn't certified to teach. None of the Los Angeles schools wanted to hire a "cripple." She tried and tried. The world around her wanted her to conform to their ideas, but she refused to. She applied at every one of the ninety school districts in the Los Angeles area. She finally got a job. They saw her potential and built ramps for her wheelchair. They waived the minor rule of having to stand before a class. Since then, Jill Kinmont has been teaching. She loves it. Her students love her. In the summers, Jill visits Indian reservations to teach reading. Jill is a life toucher because she decided to face up to the conflict.

Strategy 9: Develop Strong Relationships With Your Parents.

I received a letter from a girl several days after I spoke to her class. It said, "I attempted suicide last month, and the main reason was that I didn't like myself very much. You and my friend and my counselor are the only people who know about it. I'd like to keep it that way. I can't go to my parents because they would get very angry if they knew."

That is one of the saddest types of letters I receive. When young people and their parents hardly know each other, it is a tragedy.

I'd like to give you some steps to take in building an open and honest relationship with your parents.

1. Explain to your parents that you need a better relationship with them. Perhaps as a first reaction they will wonder if you plan on meeting them halfway. Tell them you will. If you can't do it verbally, write them a letter.
2. Tell your parents how much you love and appreciate them.

3. Ask what areas you can improve in. Have them make a list. (By doing these three steps you are showing your true desire to build a winning relationship with the two most important people in your life.)
4. In a loving, nonjudgmental way, share with them how they frustrate you. But please, *never shout!*
5. Tell them you need them most when you are in trouble. Ask them to be patient with you when you come to them with your concerns. Ask them to just listen and give no advice when you most need them to "be there" and "support" you.
6. Try to set up a regular time when you can sit and talk. If peace and quiet are hard to find, go to the doughnut shop or someplace where you can get away from the phone and house.
7. Pray about this relationship. God invented the family, and He wants to guide you to developing a loving, encouraging one.

I'm proud of you for taking the initiative to get this started. When you start to see results, you'll feel proud, too.

Strategy 10: Don't Limit Your Self-image to Your Physical Appearance and Abilities. Over 70 percent of today's youth, I'd estimate, see themselves (their self-image) in light of their looks and abilities. Don't limit your self-image (how you see yourself) and ultimately your self-esteem (how you feel about yourself) to these two areas alone. Instead develop your self-image these five ways:

1. *Discover who you really are.* First you'll need to learn to talk to yourself, just as you would a friend. In some quiet time alone, write out your feelings about things important to you, putting your fears and limitations down on paper. Write out how you have reacted in specific situations in the past and how you wish you had acted. Some effort and a little time are all you'll require. You'll get a lot out of this exercise. Many people never really discover who they are and what they are truly like. They go through their entire lives with masks on.

Bravely take yours off. Put down the truth. Although you are not perfect, you have many positive points. You can't do everything great, but you have hidden talents just waiting to be found.

2. *Concentrate on your many plusses.* When we studied your "blessed list" and "success list," we did this. Get these back out and look them over. Only if you remember them by seeing them often will you gain strength and power from them.

3. *Feel good about your beliefs.* Find out what you believe in. Start with discovering what your family believes in. What moral values do you hold dear? If you don't have any real, solid beliefs in your life, work hard to get some. It is vital that you start deciding and reaching for the truth. Only the truth will set a person free from the grip of uncertainty and fear.

The book I hold dear to my life says the Son of God is the Truth and the Light and that He is the doorway in which I must enter to reach God the Father. I've searched and searched, and now I'm totally at peace with myself and my Maker, and the people around me, because I have discovered who Bill Sanders is and what I believe in.

Decide what you believe in and stand up for it! Believe it or not, even if someone makes fun of your beliefs, you'll still live. As one teen wrote me: "I've been ridiculed for my Christian beliefs, but you showed me that it's important to stand for something and know exactly what it is. I'm proud of your stand, too." I appreciate that young person's stand, also. It takes a lot of character to face others like that. But in the long run, that young Christian won, and his ridiculers lost out.

4. *Become Closer to Your Family.* Consider this next paragraph carefully, because most young people today do not fully understand what I'm about to say.

The responsibility of what happens in your life and in the lives of other family members is often a shared responsibility. Before you can truly identify with things greater than yourself (your world, the role you play in society, God, school, work), you must learn to identify with your family. Troubled teens and most teens who get into trouble do not feel a contributing part of their family. They don't realize they have importance, and often other family members don't make them feel important. So instead of trying to be helpful, understanding family members, they "do their own thing" and explain away their differences by the age-old cop-out, "That's just the way I am, and I can't change."

Becoming closer to your family is no different from strengthening your relationship with your close friends. Sometimes you have to give in and do what your friend wants to do. Other times you have to be a good listener when he needs to talk and share something important. At times you'll know you should leave him alone or help her with her car or him with a project. It's the same with your family. Do for your family what you do for your friends, and you will be amazed at how well things go. Isn't it surprising how we often treat the most important people in our lives like dirt?

I'll always remember the influence my brother Joe had on me. One sunny summer day, working in Flint, Michigan, I helped him clean, seal coat, and stripe a large parking lot. It was dirty and very hot work. While I picked up dirt and put it in a five-gallon bucket to take off the lot, he said to me, "You know, you are one of the best workers I have ever seen." I acted as if I couldn't hear him and said, "What did you say?" He told me again, "You're a good worker. You are doing the dirtiest job on the lot, and you are doing it well. I'm proud of you." I stood a little taller that day. I felt like saying to my brother, "Yeah, I always have liked to work. It seemed like the dishes couldn't get dirty fast enough around the house, and it seems like the grass couldn't grow fast enough, because I always wanted to mow it." I didn't say those things, but I sure did feel like it. My brother told me that I was a good worker. He taught me how to sell. He taught me to get up at six in the morning and work until midnight if we had to. I'm sorry that I wasn't wise enough to tell him back then, "Thanks, Joe, for really changing my life." But since then I have always taken pride in doing a good job.

Those few words probably weren't a big thing to Joe, but they sure meant a lot to me! You can have the same kind of experience with your family, if you let yourself.

5. *Help others who need you.* People who help others generally feel better about themselves. I'm not necessarily suggesting full-time social work, however if you are best suited for this area, you'll feel happiest doing it. I *am* recommending that you look for ways to lend others a helping hand. You may help an elderly person, watch a neighbor's baby while she goes to the store, or clean out the eaves for a neighbor. Do such chores without pay, except for the self-satisfaction they give you.

Extending a helping hand doesn't mean you have to take on a large task, but the returns on it can be immense for the person you help. You don't have to do something too big for someone else to have an impact on his life. Sometimes a chance situation will give you a real influence in a life—like my registration day for my first semester at junior college. I'll never forget it!

Since my name began with the letter *S*, and everything was done in alphabetical order, I stood in one long line after another. I learned an exciting, positive thing that day: the words *section closed.* After I waited in line for about forty-five minutes to register for one of my classes, the sign came out: SECTION CLOSED. I waited in another line for about forty-five minutes and again, two in front of me, SECTION CLOSED. By that time I'd spent almost half a day there. My buddies had *all* their credit hours. I only had *one* measly physical education class, worth one credit. By this time, a whole new set of letters went up for the new batch of students coming in. Well, I made my first college decision that day: I decided to quit. I felt ashamed that I couldn't even make it through registration that day without my friends. As I was walking out with my head hung low, tail between my legs, making eye contact with no one, a warm hand touched my shoulder. A man about fifty years old said to me, "What are you doing?"

"I'm quitting," I told him without looking up.

"Quitting what?" Still walking, I answered, "Quitting college."

"This isn't college, this is registration!"

"Then I'm quitting registration."

Then he said some of the kindest words I have ever heard: "Come into my office. Let's talk about it."

I shared my story. He got some paper and asked me what classes I wanted. Then he wrote them all down on add slips. He told me that I could come in Monday and use the add slips.

I said, "Just like that?"

"Just like that. No strings attached. We need you at this school."

"You need me? I was going to quit five minutes ago. What do you mean?"

"Do you know how many students get to that door and never come back before we reach them? Do you know how many more never even come here, because they don't think they are good enough for college? You have something called empathy. You have walked in their moccasins for a mile. We need you here as long as you never forget how you felt as you were walking out. I want you to help us reach other students in this school. Students who feel ready to quit. Students who are alone and afraid. Students who might be thinking about suicide because a girl friend or boyfriend broke up with him or her, and that person thinks life isn't worth it. Students, who because they listen to so many things in their lives that tell them the importance of material things, believe that because they flunked a class, life isn't worth living."

Well, he gave me that little speech, and I guess that I was just gullible enough to believe it. For the next two years, that gave me a reason to be at school. Getting my grades alone no longer seemed so important. I was on the lookout for students who walked close to the wall, making eye contact with no one. I watched for students who ate alone in the cafeteria and for other people who hurt deep inside.

That man's name was Chuck Holland—I can hardly believe he called himself "just a counselor." I want you to know that no one is *just* an anything. In fact, if you think your garbage man is *just* a garbage man, let him leave you for about a month. Like my friend Steve and my brother Joe, Chuck Holland was a life changer and a lifesaver. Just like the Lifesavers candies you can buy in the store, they come in all colors. You can be a lifesaver to one of your friends—or even to someone you don't know. Maybe an underclassman. Maybe a friend who shouts for attention, but the world can't hear him. About sixty people that year told me that I had touched their lives in a positive way. Several said that they stayed in school because I came along at the right time. Others said they were able to cope because someone cared.

Strategy 11: Order a Reuben for a Change. The next time you go out to eat with your friends, make sure that you order the first thing you decide on. Make your own choice—order what you want. Don't ask anyone, "What are you getting?"

Most people go along with the crowd. They never develop their ability to make decisions. By making quick decisions in minor areas like ordering food, choosing school clothes, deciding how long to talk on the phone or do homework, you will prepare yourself for a possible life-and-death situation. If you can't tell the group that you don't want to participate in one of their activities, you may not live to tell about it. Thousands of teenagers have failed to tell the drunk driver, "I'm not riding with you, let me out," or to tell a friend, "I choose not to take those drugs." We read about the failures everyday in the newspapers.

Surveys taken of the strengths that make people successful, often have *decision making* right at the top of the list. At the same time, procrastination tops the list for failures. So order your own meal next time. Look at the menu, decide for yourself, then put down that menu. If you want to have some fun, just tell your friends what you are ordering and watch how many get the same thing.

Strategy 12: Take Inventory of Past Peer-Pressure Decisions. You'll get a real "eye opener" when you list how you have responded to certain situations in the past, how things turned out, and what you have learned in the process. Make a chart of the times you have gotten in trouble. Who were you with? Who was the leader? Were you drinking or taking drugs? Was it planned or did it just happen? The answers to these questions will show you who is "bad news" and who to stay away from.

A few years ago, I realized that everytime I would drink alcohol something negative happened. I would get a headache or lose money playing pool. My morals would begin breaking down right before my eyes. So I made a decision not to drink at all. By eliminating the source, I've eliminated all the negative "end results" as well.

It hurts when you find out that some people bump into trouble as easily as birds fly. You'll also hurt when you realize that you must part company and lose that friendship. Some people have stronger influences on us than we do on them, and the more we stay around them, the more likely we are to be pulled down to their level.

Strategy 13: Look at Long-term Reality. Today's popular chants include, "Do it if it feels good," and "Live for today, don't worry about tomorrow." They don't seem too realistic, but school doesn't help much either. Teachers often don't show how your studies relate to the world you live in. They only say, "You'll need this when you're older," or, "You'll be glad you studied this when you get a job." So how do you know what's best now?

As hard as it is, you must look at the long-term results of your friendships, activities, and habits. What you plant today will most surely sprout tomorrow. And tomorrow always seems to arrive sooner than you expect.

Suppose you had a new, shiny car and wanted to take it for a drive: Which road would you go on—the washboard, gravel road with the bumps and holes and loose stones or the smooth, paved road? Of course you'd pick the paved one. Why? Because you don't want your car to get ruined, and you anticipate a much better ride on the smooth road. It's the same with your life. Look at the long-term, end result and start making wise choices today.

If certain people continually make wrong choices for their lives, stay away from them or be careful while around them. If you're a girl, and a guy with a bad reputation wants to take you out on a date, you had better be extra careful. Better yet, say no. The odds are that he isn't planning on holding hands all evening.

If you want to earn and save a lot of money, don't associate with people who have a knack for getting fired from their jobs. If you want to be a person of integrity, don't become best friends with thieves or liars.

Look at reality and think about what'll happen a year or two down the road. The outcome of your activities and habits should be of great importance to you today. The activities, friends, beliefs, and habits you carry today will determine the "you" in the future.

Strategy 14: Develop Faith in Your Ability to Solve Your Own Problems. As a teen, when you face problems (a broken home, a breakup with girl friend or boyfriend, loneliness, flunking out of school, loss of job, no hope for the future, and so on), you have three basic ways you can face them:

1. Let others decide what to do about this problem (usually your parents or peer group).
2. Escape from the problem by pretending it isn't there any longer (using drugs or alcohol, wasting time and money with your friends).
3. Solve the problem yourself (those who have had ample opportunities to solve problems as they are growing up do well as teens).

Most young people haven't developed the skill in solving their own problems for one of these reasons:

1. They have never learned that they have—thus they don't believe they have—the resources within themselves to handle their problems.
2. They don't believe they determine the outcome of their lives. They feel life is made up of "luck," "chance," or "things outside yourself."
3. Most of today's youth have never had to "do without." Therefore, when faced with a situa-

tion in which they lose something, they think something is wrong. For example: If clothes, toys, a new bike when I want it, are given to me throughout my childhood, I don't know what it's like to "do without" things. Then, when my dog dies and my girl friend breaks up with me, I think there is something wrong with me.

4. The media say don't worry about problem solving—it will all turn out okay by next week's episode. But real life can't be like a sitcom, no matter how hard you try to make it one.

5. Most parents solve the problems for their kids. They don't want their child to go through the tough times they did. They don't understand that they only prolong the time for their child to stumble and fall as they go through the learning process.

You can develop problem-solving skills and counteract these five root causes to the problem by following these guidelines:

1. Learn to solve the little problems first. Solve at least one problem a day. It may only be to rearrange your clothes in your closet so you can find things more easily. But if it saves you time and effort, you have just solved a problem. Or write down what you are going to wear to school for an entire week. You will have eliminated any need to worry about clothes all next week.

   Make a list of some small and large problems you face. Ask for help from those who can solve their own problems. Remember: It's better to do something, even if it's wrong, than to do nothing at all. You won't *always* do it right—that's okay. Part of problem solving is developing the right attitude. Be a person who says, "I'm not perfect, but I'm doing pretty well, and I'm doing it myself."

2. Realize that life is made up of cause and effect. What you do causes what will happen to you. I realize there is what some people might call a

"luck factor," but I also believe luck is what happens to a person when he has worked hard and prepared for what is ahead of him. Students who get A's work hard for A's. Students who make the team have earned the right. NASA doesn't pick astronauts alphabetically. They study and plan and put forth effort. Cause and effect. We get out of life what we put into it. Don't fool yourself by saying life is made up of chance or luck or accident. Be like the ant. He works hard in the summer to get ready for the winter. He doesn't look at his work haphazardly. Don't gamble with the outcome of your grades or friendships. If you fail a grade, don't blame the lottery: You chose to fail. You chose it when you didn't put forth the needed work and discipline to study.

3. Make yourself do without things that are important to you. This will make you a stronger person. It will also show you that life isn't one giant bowl of berries. It's perfectly normal to work and not have. It will prepare you to save your money and not buy impulse items. Don't go with the gang if you haven't done your homework. Don't party if you have important things that should get done.

I was in bed at 10:00 P.M. on my eighteenth birthday. Many of my friends wanted me to go party with them. I would have loved to, but I had my own business and a big job to do at 6:00 A.M. the next morning. It was hard, but I became stronger for it.

4. The media, especially TV, are in many ways far from reality. The hero doesn't always arrive in the nick of time to save the day for those less fortunate. People don't have smiles on their faces and respect from others when they treat people the way J.R. does. You don't get ahead in business by stepping on others. You'll never be able to snap your finger and get the girls the way the Fonz does.

Many TV shows (especially the soaps) do as well as they do because millions of viewers can't solve their own problems and believe life is out to get them, so they wallow in the misery of the actors on the tube.

5. Ask your parents (lovingly) not to solve your problems. As a teen, you are a young adult— even if you don't feel that way. If you're an average teen, your parents treat you like a child, yet quite often they want you to act as responsibly as an adult. Talk to them. Don't resent them. Work it out. Level with them. Tell them how important it is for you to learn to make decisions and mistakes while you live at home. In this way, you can gain the experience you need to live on your own and handle the world once you move out. If you get behind on your paper route, don't let your dad always do it for you. (It's okay once in a while.) Take the responsibility and do it, even if you are tired or have a headache. Or go to the newspaper company and tell them face-to-face you can't do it anymore. The same with buying a bike or a car—don't ask your parents to buy it for you or even to cosign a loan. Get it on your own or don't get it.

Make your own decisions. You can do it. Remember: The effort put forth now will aid you the rest of your life.

Strategy 15: Replace Blame with Responsibility. As the last strategy for overcoming peer pressure, let's look at two words: *blame* and *responsibility*. First, let's look at blame. Blame will lead you toward misery and worry and a life of make-believe— a life in which you convince yourself that your problems aren't really yours at all. "It's his fault." "My teacher just doesn't understand." Some people blame everyone. There are several all-time favorite "blame targets": Parents rate high on the list; so do the government, the president, the principal, and the weather.

People who blame others have never learned that life is a

cause-and-effect situation. We cause our outcomes by our actions, preparations, and hard or soft work. Blaming is a cop-out. It says, "Nothing works out for me," and, "Everyone is out to get me." Blame focuses on the past and others and keeps your mind off your positive future. Blame stunts growth and encourages people to wallow in their misery.

Now for the second word: *responsibility*. Replace blame with this. Take full credit for your success and failure. I've heard many successful people say, "I'm a self-made success." But I've never heard a failure say, "I'm a self-made failure." Why? People don't like to admit when they goofed up or didn't study hard enough or weren't prepared.

If you have held others responsible for any of your problems, forgive them. Then go to them and tell them you no longer blame them. *Forgiveness is the key.* You must totally forgive a person who has wronged, betrayed, or lied to you. By forgiving him, you lift the weight of blame from your shoulders.

I know of a twenty-five-year-old man who still blames his parents for every problem he has ever had. He was the first child. When his other brothers and sisters came along, he wasn't number one any more. He became the problem teenager, and his parents never knew how to say no. They bought his car and bailed him out of jail. They came to his rescue time and time again. He still calls home almost weekly, asking for money to make it through another few days. Guess what? They still send the money. They actually encourage and prolong his behavior. If he could just forgive them for what he feels (even if they actually did wrong him), he could totally escape the damaging effect of this blaming way of life.

When I counsel inmates in prison, I rarely find one who takes full responsibility for his life and the results of his actions. So please get out of the blame prison and enjoy the freedom only taking responsibility will give you.

Making These Strategies Work in Your Life

Now you have the head knowledge to make the most of your life by fighting back against peer pressure. But it's up to you to really put these fifteen strategies to work in your life. I can't do it for you. Your parents or counselor can't do it for you Al though it *will* take work, I know you *can* do it.

Start practicing these steps today—don't put it off! Sure you won't be able to make every change overnight. Tomorrow you won't be perfect—but you can be better. By the end of a week you'll have done even more. And imagine what your life could be like at the end of a year!

It's never an easy battle. But those who do fight against peer pressure will be better for it. The results of your decisions now can touch your whole life.

Make your life terrific. Start today! In these chapters you have all the basics. Some people in your life really care for you. Seek them out; get close to them. Make the most of what *you* have—be yourself!

Check Out Your Turf

1. Which strategies listed here have you already used to fight peer pressure? How have you used them in specific situations?
2. What strategies do you need to use that you have not made a part of your life? How could you use them effectively?
3. How can you begin to become closer to others (your family, friends, and others whom you might be able to help)? Name three ways you could do this.
4. As you have been reading this book have you begun to make changes in the way you handle peer pressure? Name some situations you have used these techniques in or some in which you need to use them.

Part 3
DRUG TURF

-8-

WHAT ARE DRUGS?

Finally, let's take a look at two of the biggest influences on teens today: drugs and alcohol. In the last twenty years a great deal of research has become available on drugs. Here I have saved you from sifting through books, pamphlets, newsletters, and cassettes by doing that for you and presenting the information, including the latest findings, in an easy-to-understand, fast-food manner. I believe you will truly be amazed and startled, as I was, at what drugs *really do* to those who get involved in them.

From the next three chapters you will be equipped with enough up-to-date, factual information to lead a class discussion, write a term paper, or start a peer-to-peer awareness program on drugs in your school or town. You will get the answers you need and deserve on what drugs are; which are the most addictive; how long after they take drugs people are affected; how drugs affect the brain, the reproductive parts, schoolwork, and chromosomes. We will look at why people take drugs and how some get off drugs. We will also read several interviews I've had with people who have taken drugs and see firsthand how their lives have drastically changed.

So What Is a Drug?

My dictionary defines a *drug* as: 1. A substance used as medicine in the treatment of disease. 2. A narcotic, especially one that is addictive.

From this description, you can see that it is not necessarily a negative word. We can use drugs for good or bad. They can save lives or ruin them. Under an ethical doctor's advice and prescription, drugs can prolong life and help families and individuals enjoy long, fulfilling existences. But used unwisely, they can lead to ruined careers, broken homes, crime, murder, and suicide.

For our purpose, let's call drugs addictive agents—things that stimulate or depress. That's a simple, fairly inclusive definition.

Drugs and Youth

Before we look at some teenagers and discuss why they "take" and "do" drugs, let me share exactly where I'm coming from concerning drug use and *you*!

I am against the use of *any* drug (except as prescribed by a doctor) by young people going through puberty or adolescence. You are in puberty until you become physiologically capable of sexual reproduction. We call this period of physical and psychological development from puberty to maturity adolescence. Of course, maturity doesn't "just happen" at age eighteen or twenty-one—or even by forty.

You are probably asking yourself, *How does he know if I'm mature?* or, *When will I know when I'm mature?* Hopefully today you have more maturity than you did a year ago. Maturity, the kind I'm referring to, physical and psychological, won't happen to you until you have completed adolescence.

In my opinion, most people leave adolescence around the ages of eighteen to twenty-one. However, this doesn't mean they are mature. Maturity is a process. Let's compare it to wisdom. We don't become wise on Wednesday; we keep becoming wiser day by day and year by year. Maturity works the same way.

You know you are becoming more mature when your logic and the way you reason things out is consistent and sound. Illogic says something like this:

> *Teenager:* "I moved out so my parents would have one less mouth to feed."
> *Friend:* "Your family must miss you."
> *Teenager:* "No, I see them every evening, when I go home for dinner."

A mature person says, "Based on the harm drugs have done to other people I have read about and know personally, I am staying away from them completely."

An immature person says, "I don't care what drugs have done to other people. I'm gonna get high tonight and forget about my troubles."

As these two examples point out, maturity looks beyond today's pleasures and focuses on tomorrow's possibilities.

What Drugs Do to You

A most critical time for a young person is the time from puberty to middle adolescence. This time in your life and drugs don't mix because changes are happening to your body, your mind, and your emotions. You can feel these changes. It's normal to be afraid or uncertain and feeling not completely in control of yourself. When you add drugs to this time of transformation, you can have a very dangerous situation with long-term effects.

As I share my findings from experts' research on youth and drugs, I'm not going to state pages or chapters or list bibliographies. For one thing, you would be bored with it. For another, you most likely wouldn't look up the references. Finally, if you trust me so far, you'll believe me. If you don't, you won't. There will be a list of books and free materials at the end of this section that are recommended reading.

Using drugs during adolescence can:

- Affect you psychologically for years to come.
- Alter your physical growth and maturing process.
- Have a negative effect on your studies, as you can be negatively affected intellectually as well.
- Alter your brain functions.
- Cause you to be very moody. (This stays with young people for many years to come.)
- Keep you from facing reality and make you live in a sort of dream world.
- Keep you from having a desire to learn.
- Keep you from coping with your problems effectively.

Your body and mind, especially if you have made a spiritual commitment to God, are a temple, a house, a place for God to dwell. Life is sacred. He did not mean it to be prostituted for money. Neither will He condone your experimenting with it by using this stimulant or that depressant just because you want to put a mask over reality and hide from the truth. Drugs offer short-term highs with possible long-term lows. Short-term successes and possible long-term failures. Drugs are short-term, but their effects are often long-term! Don't forget it. Wait until I share my interviews with Kevin and Gary if you don't believe people suffer from these long-term hurts and regrets.

Why Do People Use Drugs?

As you probably already realize and as you will see in the next pages, people take drugs for all kinds of reasons. However, the usual ones fall under a few main headings.

1. Low self-esteem
2. Peer-group pressure
3. Family problems
4. The need to be accepted
5. Avoiding reality
6. "Getting even" with significant others

Below are statements young people have shared with me and other researchers as to why they do drugs:

"I never wanted to smoke even one joint, let alone get high every day, but I was offered a joint at a blast [party] by a neat chick, and I couldn't refuse it. I've been smoking ever since."

"In our school if you aren't a jock or an Einstein, you're a nerd. I don't fit in. I'm not a druggie. I just do drugs all the time."

"Everybody I know smokes dope. I bet ninety percent of the kids in this school do it. I'm just doing what everyone else does. What's wrong with that?"

"When I get high it's like there's no school, no zits, and no worries. It's just me and no one bugging me. It's great. Besides, it's not hurting anything."

"My parents drink booze every time they go out to dinner or have friends over. So I drink and do dope. What's the difference? They're both drugs, and they both can get you wasted."

"Ever since my dad left home we don't have much of a family. My mom's out just about every night, trying to get picked up at a bar. I've got to stay here and baby-sit. It makes me sick, and it's not fair. I've been doing PCP and booze for about a year. It seems to help."

"When we would double date, I was the only one who didn't share a joint when it was passed around. My boyfriend kept telling me I was weird and that it wouldn't hurt me, so I tried it. I didn't even get high the first time. Now I smoke more than him. I probably smoke about five joints during the week and five on the weekend."

"I've already found out I didn't receive that scholarship. I'll probably end up a factory rat or something. Doing drugs just seems to help, that's all."

"I hate it when people tell me what to do. If they would say it nicely, that's one thing, but my parents have a way of ordering me around that drives me crazy. I don't care what they say; I'll smoke pot as long as I want."

"My boyfriend and I have been having sex for two years

now, since I was fourteen. We both know it's wrong, but we're deeply in love. When we get high it's like it's okay."

"When my dad got transferred here for his job, I told him I didn't want to leave. I hate it here. The kids are pure weirdo. Most of them don't like me either. I get along with one group, and they turned me on to drugs. Besides, my parents are too busy to care. I sneak out my window sometimes, and they don't have the foggiest idea."

The people just interviewed come in all shapes and sizes. They look like you and me. They get average grades and good grades. They come from rich and poor families, from every possible religious background. Drugs have a grip on millions of people.

I've had the opportunity to speak to teenagers, their parents, and school administrators all across America, from Alaska to Florida and from New York to California. I've spoken in small communities in North Dakota, to huge inner-city schools like those in Detroit, and I can tell you firsthand, drugs are everywhere.

In the next chapters we'll take a look at specific drugs and the results of using them. We'll talk with some people who have been there and know what it's like, and we'll hear their stories.

Checking Out Your Turf

1. What is a drug? How are drugs meant to be used? How do people use them?

2. What does *maturity* really mean? How will you know when you are becoming mature? How have you grown in maturity in the past year? What areas do you need to grow in?

3. List some of the effects drugs can have on you. What would these mean for you long-term? What reasons do people give for using drugs? Will they really help in any of these situations? Why or why not?

-9-

KEEP OFF THE GRASS

I once spoke at a youth leadership conference to student leaders from all the area high schools—you might call them the "cream of the crop." Each school sent their top four or five student leaders to participate in my seminars and meetings. At the end of the day, when the program was over, a girl came up to me and shared that she felt like a hypocrite. She told me how she and about ninety percent of the other students got stoned on marijuana during the lunch break. These same leaders had told me they planned to "make a difference" at their schools and encourage other students to set goals, believe in themselves, avoid peer pressure, say no to drugs, and so on.

I asked, "Why would you leaders jeopardize all you have going for you by breaking the law and exposing your bodies to a damaging substance such as marijuana?"

"Oh, don't get me wrong," she answered. "We're not druggies. We aren't addicted or anything. We just get a buzz on the weekends and sometimes on lunch hours. Besides, everyone smokes weed these days, and it isn't like it's heroin or something. Marijuana is harmless, isn't it?" I thanked her for her honesty and willingness to share with me.

She used the cop-out many kids in your school use for doing drugs: "Everyone else is." Don't forget the common reason why people take drugs. In most cases it starts out to be socially accepted. But the reason they keep taking them are:

1. Low self-esteem: *If I don't like me, I sure don't care what I smoke or drink or shoot up.*
2. Family problems and getting even with significant others: *I'm the black sheep in this family. My parents don't want to know when I'm in trouble or need help. We just can't talk. I don't have a future anyway. I might as well do drugs.*
3. The need to be accepted: *Everyone is at parties smoking and drinking. How are you supposed to make friends if you don't go along with the crowd?*
4. Avoiding reality: *There's no future for my generation. Nuclear war is one thing, but there are no jobs out there for another. If I don't at least have a 3.5 average this year, college is out of the question. My parents will kill me. All I do is drink. It helps me forget all the garbage in my life.*
5. Peer-group acceptance: *They didn't really make me smoke a joint with them. They just made it very clear I'd never be a part of their group if I didn't do what they did. I guess I needed their friendship a lot, because I've paid a big price for it. It seems my motivation for school and my job is completely gone.*

Hard-Core Facts About Drug Abuse

Please notice that I call it "drug abuse" not "drug use." Drug use means using prescribed drugs in the way they were meant to be used: by a doctor, in the right quantities, at the right times, and so on. Drug abuse is what people do when they take illegal drugs or overuse legal ones. They don't know the makeup of the substance they are putting in their bodies, or the short- or long-term effects the drug will have on them, or how it will affect those around them, their work, their brains, their memory, and so on. Drug abuse means abusing your body and the drug. So drug users are really drug abusers and body bruisers. When you use marijuana, you're involved in *drug abuse.*

Before you defend its use, think a bit about these facts:

> Marijuana is the second most widely used drug among teenagers today. (We'll talk about number one in a later chapter.)
> Grass (another name for marijuana) is sold *daily* in elementary, junior high, and high schools. (If you're thinking about doing it, first ask yourself if you'd like to have your younger brother or sister doing it.)
> Ninety percent of the hard-core addicts (such as heroin users) started with marijuana.

Despite these facts, young people everywhere say, "Smoking pot can't hurt you." "It's not as bad as booze." "I've been smoking for several years, and I'm okay." We'll look closely at the latest findings on marijuana to see exactly what happens to thousands of pot users. Ignorance is no excuse when it comes to ruining your own life. Listen in as a group of teenagers asks me questions about marijuana. They were startled at some of my answers, based on research scientists have done for more than twenty-five years. Here it goes:

Q: How many students are smoking grass today?

A: It's estimated that over 80 percent of today's high-school seniors have tried marijuana.

Q: What actually causes a person to get high when smoking marijuana?

A: THC (Tetrahydrocannabinol), a strong and misunderstood chemical. The higher the percentage of THC, the stronger the marijuana.

Q: How strong is the marijuana that is around today, compared to that of ten years ago?

A: The THC in today's marijuana is ten to twenty times more powerful than just ten years ago.

Q: How does THC give you a high?

A: It goes to the pleasure center of your brain.

Q: How bad is the dope scene today?

A: It's estimated that anywhere from 60 percent to 80 percent of all high school graduates have tried pot at least once. About ten percent of all high school seniors are daily pot smokers. Twenty to forty billion dollars a year is spent on marijuana.

Q: What parts of the body does THC do the most damage to?

A: The brain, lungs, and the reproductive organs. These areas are loaded with fat, and THC loves fat!

Q: How much THC is in marijuana?

A: In the 1960s there was less than 1 percent THC in marijuana. Today there is over 6 percent, and there can be up to twenty times as much as just ten years ago. This means the damage (long- and short-term) is estimated to be much greater also.

Q: What else is in marijuana?

A: Over 431 different chemicals. In fact, this is the main reason why it's been so hard to study and learn all about what this drug actually does to people.

Q: Do you consider marijuana a dangerous drug?

A: *Yes!* Marijuana is the most dangerous drug biologically because it affects every cell in the body, settles in the fatty cells, and destroys so many millions of cells, making it easier for the user to get diseases.

Q: Can you get hooked on pot?

A: You sure can. Studies show that 45 percent of all the people who ever get involved with pot will become addicted. One man shared this analogy with me about drug addiction. He asked me if I would get on an airplane if I knew that four out of every ten planes that took off would crash? I said, "Of course not." He said, "That's what people do when they smoke pot. Four out of every ten will become addicted."

Q: Why don't more people act alarmed at all the marijuana use today?

A: There are many reasons for this. For a long time we knew very little about it. Today scientists have written over 8,500 papers on their marijuana research. Now we know about many of the dangers we only suspected just ten years ago. The head shops (shops that sell drug paraphernalia) and magazines such as *High Times* have been making money from drugs for years, and they have said it was harmless. Today head shops are forbidden in forty states. Our country is getting fed up with this outrageous drug culture. It destroys our most valuable resource—our young people—tomorrow's only future!

Q: Can I get high if I'm at a party where others are smoking, if I'm not?

A: Yes. Research has found these two things to be true: (1) If you breathe in the pot smoke from the other smokers, THC will show up in your blood; (2) if you breathe enough smoke, you can get just as high as the pot smokers themselves. It's called a "contact high."

Q: Does smoking grass affect a person's driving?

A: It sure does. People's reaction time is proven to slow down when they are high. Pot smokers can't react as fast during emergencies and are more likely to be involved in an accident than people who are straight.

Q: If a person gets stoned at a party, and two hours later he comes down from the high, will he be able to drive as though he never got high?

A: No, because it takes about six hours after the high for him to regain all his reflexes. The slow reactions last longer than the buzz. It looks as though that big Mack truck is only going twenty miles per hour, when it's actually going sixty.

Q: Why do doctors and experts tell pregnant women not to smoke pot?

A: Because the THC goes through the mother's blood system, right into the unborn child. Actually, the THC goes straight to the baby's brain and can have a devastating effect on the child, because it stays there for weeks and causes a chemical imbalance and abnormal growth in the baby.

Q: Why do teachers say they can tell if students are on dope when they are in class?

A: Because pot smoking causes poor memory, loss of willpower, a feeling of paranoia, and a lack of ambition. All these add up to poor grades. Teachers, parents, and doctors are starting to learn the following symptoms of pot smokers:

School-Related Problems That Affect
Most Marijuana Users

1. Assignments turned in late.
2. Tardiness, excuses, more passes, and forged notes.
3. Out-of-school absences on the rise, especially on Monday and Friday.
4. Inconsistent work in the classroom.
5. Sloppy handwriting.
6. An "I don't care" attitude.
7. More errors than ever before—even on simple items.
8. Grades going down and offering no thoughts during classroom discussions.
9. Leaving school-sponsored events and then returning later.
10. Tired in class and sleeping during school hours.
11. Avoiding teachers, principal, and all authority figures.

Q: Can pot smoking cause cancer?

A: Yes. One joint is equal to 112 tobacco cigarettes because of all the cancer-causing hydrocarbons in pot.

Q: Do you feel our lawmakers should legalize marijuana to make it less of a danger to our society?

A: Absolutely not. Look what happened by legalizing alcohol. It's the number-one killer of teens, when mixed with driving. Legalizing alcohol hasn't kept it out of the hands of young people—it's only made it worse. We surely don't need any more stupefying drugs in our society, whether they are legal or illegal.

Q: If alcohol and tobacco are so harmful, why are they legal and marijuana isn't?

A: Because those drugs were legalized years before enough data had been collected or complex research had been gathered, stating the dangers of both of these addictive drugs.

Q: What does it mean to get hooked on drugs?

A: It depends on your tolerance level. How much of the drug does a person need in order to get high and stay high? Alcoholics, for instance, need more and more alcohol to get the same feeling as they once did. Heavy pot smokers need more THC to get high.

A month-long test proved that when someone smokes pot several times a day, he barely feels a high off ten joints a day. After a great deal of drug use, your body actually learns to burn up the drug faster, therefore you need more of the drug for the same effect.

You know you are hooked on *anything* when you have compulsive reactions such as these:

1. You must rob and steal in order to buy more drugs.
2. You drive to a store in the middle of the night to get a cigarette.
3. You buy a new TV just to see your favorite TV show when your old one is being repaired.
4. You tear your room apart or search for hours in your car trying to find an old roach. (What's left from a used joint.)

Being hooked and building a tolerance level has nothing to do with your brain. It is simply a part of drug use. Don't start if you don't want to take a chance and get hooked.

When a person is hooked on a drug (cigarettes, pot, alcohol, heroin, cocaine, caffeine) and quits, he goes through withdrawal symptoms such as: cramps, shivering, nausea, vomiting, insomnia, nervousness, and irritability. Just because people don't go into screaming fits when they quit marijuana doesn't mean it isn't addicting. As mentioned before, about 40 percent of all those who ever smoke a joint will become addicted. THC is a very dangerous chemical that easily leads to dependency by the user.

Signs of Pot Smokers

1. Avoid teachers, parents, other family members, and church members.
2. Hang around a new group of peers.
3. Seem to be with "others" all the time—never alone. Being alone is not comfortable at all.
4. Fighting behavior is increased.
5. Exhibit loud, raucous behavior, belligerent, and hostile.
6. Move from group to group, changing friends often.
7. Abuse others' rights.
8. Family seems miles away. Afraid to get close to loved ones.
9. Paranoid when authority figures are around.
10. Overreacts to ordinary situations.
11. Mood changes often.
12. No goals or direction.
13. Frustrated easily.
14. Increased number of fears.
15. Feeling of inferiority.
16. Becoming passive.
17. Ignore responsibilities.
18. Active, defensive, and angry.
19. Need others to make decisions for them.

Most people who abuse drugs:

1. Don't see the importance of personal hygiene. They don't dress neatly, and hair and grooming goes downhill.
2. Skip meals often.
3. Change eating habits often. Lots of junk food to keep up with the munchies.

4. Wear clothes that show rebellion.
5. Change their sleeping habits.
6. Catch some illnesses easily.
7. Have a change in complexion.
8. Often have bloodshot eyes.
9. Find it harder to concentrate.
10. Take a "who cares" attitude toward life in general.
11. Become easily depressed.
12. Often think of suicide as a "way out."
13. Have very little spiritual emphasis on life.
14. Become very private—locked drawers.
15. Leave joints in shirts, car, or room, becoming very careless.
16. Look at lying as justified.
17. Often have new acquaintances appear around home.
18. Deny drug usage or possibility of being hooked.
19. Sometimes carry weapons of defense to protect themselves.

But It's Only Pot

Facts and figures make it all look so simple. But let's remember what we're talking about here is lives—people who have been destroyed or harmed by the effects of drugs on their systems.

Kevin is twenty-eight years old. He is married, has a great job, a beautiful wife and home, lots of friends, is active in his church, and spends a great deal of time playing sports and working with teens. Sounds like he's got it all together, right? Well, he does. *Now,* that is. But it wasn't always that way for Kevin.

In his sophomore year Kevin moved from a very large school, where he was just a scared, shy kid among thousands, to a rather small school where he became the starting quarterback and number-one baseball player. He loved the change. He had two of the best years of his life. Everyone knew he was a stand-out in sports. His girl friend was captain of the cheerleaders. What could be better?

Kevin used to go to parties with a Dr. Pepper in his hand. Everyone knew he was good at sports, so they never offered him drugs or booze.

During his senior year he was scouted by the Chicago White Sox. One of their top scouts watched Kevin play several games. Because Kevin was one of the best hitters and fielders Michigan had ever produced, the people from the Sox were impressed. They wanted him to start in the minor leagues and work his way up.

First they wanted Kevin to experience college ball and arranged with a small college in Michigan that he would receive a scholarship, so he could go to school and play baseball. Kevin felt so happy as he realized what a great opportunity he had.

But an incident a few weeks after he graduated almost ruined Kevin's life. He went to a party where everyone was drinking or smoking pot. Kevin had never done either and felt afraid that he would lose his scholarship if he was found doing them. When a girl offered him a toke on a joint, he said, "No way!" He hadn't tried it and wasn't going to start. She told him it was her birthday, and if he would take just one "hit," she would be happy. Kevin kept saying no, and the girl kept pressuring him.

Finally he said, "I won't smoke it here, because I might be embarrassed, but if you'll let me take it home, I'll try it tomorrow, when I'm all alone." It was, he admits today, the worst decision of his life.

He could have thrown it away, but Kevin was curious about what it was like and felt he owed it to the girl to try it. He smoked that joint and realized it hadn't killed him. He hardly got "high." He didn't even know what the word meant. So that week he bought some more marijuana and started getting high every day. A few weeks later he tried acid, which gave him a stronger high. By the end of the summer, he was doing cocaine. It all started with one joint.

Kevin told the college to go jump in a lake and was too stoned the opening day of school to even show up. It took him four years to get off drugs, and that didn't happen until he became a Christian, asking Jesus to take over his life.

Today Kevin feels that by making that decision to do drugs, he let his family down, let himself down, and in a way let God down. After all, God gave him his sports abilities. He still thinks of what could have happened. Now he'll never know how good he could have become.

When I asked Kevin where he thought he went wrong, he told me, "I had enough confidence to say no, but I didn't have enough smarts to get away from the temptation. I tell the teens today to walk away from the temptation. Don't stick around and let it wear you down, as it did me."

Kevin is trying to make some good come from his story. He shares it in churches, in youth groups, wherever people will listen. Kevin's story didn't have a tragic ending, compared to some, but who is to say what tragedy really is? You see, I know how much it hurts him, because he is one of my very best friends.

Checking Out Your Turf

1. What are some of the reasons why teens use pot? What kind of thinking goes into such a decision?

2. What does *drug abuse* mean? When is drug use *not* drug abuse?

3. What are some of the facts you learned about marijuana? Why is it dangerous? What influence will it have on your schoolwork? What will it do to your spiritual life?

4. What are some of the signs of a pot smoker? What do they show about the life of the person who uses marijuana?

5. What did you learn from Kevin's story? Do you think his story is unusual? Why or why not?

-10-

WHAT ABOUT OTHER DRUGS?

There are lots of different kinds of drugs. We could spend whole books discussing each kind and the results from taking it, but we won't here. I'll just give you some of the shocking facts I found in my research.

Marijuana may be the most dangerous drug, because it affects every cell in the body and 40 percent of the people who use it become addicted.

Cocaine is the most addictive drug in our society.

LSD (acid) is so potent that twelve ounces of the drug would be enough to send 14 million people on a trip.

Two percent of the heroin or cocaine addicts become completely cured. The rest die or end up in jail because of the crimes they commit to pay for their habits. Some even end up in mental institutions.

PCP (angel dust) ranks as the third most widely used drug among teens. This horse tranquilizer is the most dangerous drug of which to take one hit. Many have never recovered from their first one.

Other drugs? Add to the list Quaaludes, speed, uppers (stimulants) and downers (depressants), amphetamines, sleeping pills, cigarettes, and a hundred others—right on down the line to airplane glue—and you have a huge national problem. Isn't it funny that with such a complex, wide-ranging problem, all you have to learn is how to say no!

Let's take a quick look at the most addictive drug, in comparison to some of the others.

Cocaine's Effects

Here is the addiction rate for:

Alcohol: 15 percent of everyone who ever takes a drink will become addicted.
Opiates (such as heroin and morphine): 70 percent become addicted.
Cocaine: 80 percent will become addicted.

That's right. Eight out of every ten people who ever mess with cocaine will become addicted. If we apply our airplane-crash comparison, that's eight crashes out of every ten! Do you see why we call people dopes when they mess with it?

What happens if you take cocaine? When it goes into a person's system, it goes to the brain's pleasure center, just like marijuana. It flushes out a chemical in this area called copamine, which causes the pleasurable high. Here's the bad part. The cocaine chemicals left in the brain cause a severe imbalance of cells, which leaves the person in a state of depression. This is why people become psychologically addicted. Pleasure and then pain and over and over again. Cocaine addicts need it every fifteen to twenty minutes. In 1980, actress Mackenzie Phillips spent over $1 million on cocaine. Now she spends much of her time telling groups of students and adults of the dangers of drugs.

More Drug Facts

Let's have another question-and-answer-session, this time about drugs other than marijuana. What are they? How do they work? Let's see.

Q: What do people mean when they talk about "illicit drug use"?

A: They mean using a drug that is illegal, using a legal drug for something other than what it was meant for, or using a substance that usually isn't thought of as a drug to induce a druglike state: glue, aerosols, paint, and so on.

Q: What's a psychoactive drug?

A: These drugs change your feelings, your behavior, and your perceptions. There are seven types of psychoactive drugs:

1. Narcotics (opium, morphine, heroin, codeine). These addictive drugs influence the senses, making the user feel a sense of euphoria. They are usually used as painkillers.
2. Sedatives (barbiturates and tranquilizers). Depressants such as these relax the user, when small doses are taken. Larger doses cause sleep.
3. Stimulants (cocaine, caffeine, amphetamines). They stimulate the central nervous system (the brain and spinal column).
4. Hallucinogens (mescaline, LSD, MDA, STP). Such mind-altering drugs have a strong effect on the central nervous system, changing the way the brain functions and causing hallucinations of sight and sound.
5. Inhalants (amyl nitrate, poppers, or nitrous oxide). Users abuse these because of the feeling of well-being they produce.
6. Alcohol. This acts as a depressant on the central nervous system.
7. Tobacco. Nicotine affects the central nervous system as well as the brain's pleasure center, causing a need for an ongoing supply to the system.

Alcohol and tobacco are legal and widely used. Many people forget or do not know they are psychoactive drugs. They often get called social drugs because they are so widely used in social situations.

Q: I've heard about look-alike drugs. What are they?

A: Look-alike drugs are pills that look like the real thing, but aren't. Drug dealers will sell anything to make a profit. If they can lie and sell a cheaper (fake) drug (look alike), they will. People build up a tolerance to the look alikes; then when they get the real thing, it's easy to have an overdose.

If you know of students who are regularly using or trafficking in drugs, you have a responsibility to get them help before they ruin their entire lives and those of many others in the process. Talk to them. Reason with them . . . show them this book. Tell them you care for them and that's why you are so concerned for their well-being. If they won't listen, go to your school counselor or tell an adult who is sensitive and concerned for people your age. You need to keep them from wrecking their lives or the lives of countless others. What if a ten-year-old buys drugs from one and has an overdose and dies? You could have stopped it, if you had the courage to tell someone.

Is It Worth It?

He was my very best friend ever since we met in fourth grade. We just really hit it off. We seemed to have so many things in common: enjoying the same sports, goofing off, building huts, riding bikes, and girls. Because we also have opposite personality traits, in many ways, our friendship has lasted to this day. I was cautious, but he dared to do anything. While I felt afraid of my own shadow, he would take the bully on in a fight. It seems I never got caught when I did wrong things, but he always did. I always got off, and he always got blamed.

Well, my friend had all the talents of a gifted athlete. In fact, everyone in our town knew he could go on to play college basketball or baseball, if he only applied himself. He also had a great sense of humor. He could make anyone laugh anytime he tried.

In about tenth grade I noticed he started to change. Now my best friend always hung around with the wrong crowd and sneaked out at night, often having to cover up this or that. I know it's normal for a sixteen-year-old to have a girl friend, but his relationship with his girl seemed like nothing I'd ever seen or will ever see again. He lived and breathed for her. He would write her ten-page poems, telling of his love for her. He would skip school to see her if she was home sick. He would walk twenty miles in the rain only to find she wasn't home, and then he would walk back.

Well, my buddy started to drink and smoke dope in school, and before you knew it, he was suspended and then kicked out in the twelfth grade.

Several years passed, and he went to Vietnam. He returned only to find his high-school sweetheart had married and now had a beautiful baby girl. He didn't care. He did all he could to get her back. He finally got her to get a divorce, and he married her. I was his best man. He told me how happy he finally felt, but I knew something was wrong. He still did drugs, only now he did anything he could get his hands on, from PCP to coke.

They had a beautiful little boy. My friend had a good job, and life seemed as if it could finally become normal for them. But he never stopped hanging around with the wrong crowd, nor did he ever stop getting high.

One night, as he and his family were sleeping, a noise woke him. He and his wife saw the dark form of a person in their house. All of a sudden my friend heard a loud "bang." It was a gun. His wife lay dead. It was over a $2,000.00 dope deal. No one knows all the details, but they aren't important. She was killed because of one joint and one drink—the ones that started my friend on this life-style.

A short time later his little boy was taken away from him and put up for adoption because the state considered my friend an unfit parent. He was an alcoholic by this time and addicted to several drugs.

Please realize something. He was a very normal person with his likes and dislikes. Drugs ruined him and his life.

He was later sent to prison. Depressed about his life, just

before his time was up he smoked a joint. He got caught and had to stay in prison one more year.

Every time he was in trouble or hurting inside and needing someone to talk to, he called me. I always came, and I always enjoyed helping out any way I could. I've laughed with him, I've cried with him, I've hurt with him. I've seen what drugs are all about. I've seen the results of disobeying authority and thinking that life doesn't repay you for your actions. I took his clothes to him after he got out of prison.

He has said that if this story could help even one person from going through the pain he has, it will be worth it. He wants you to know that he has put his faith in God and has replaced the word *blame* with *responsibility*. He has taken full responsibility for all his actions and outcomes. He has a nightmare to live with, and now he is trying to make something good come from his life. We thought it would be best not to use his name, as he has already hurt enough—besides, he doesn't want any recognition. He just wants you to realize that life can't take a joke. If you play with fire, you're going to get burned. Don't think it can't happen to you—my friend's story proves it *can*.

What About Drug Trends?

Thirty years ago, if you were a teen, your peers pressured you into smoking cigarettes. My dad told me that people used to make fun of those who didn't smoke on the job. Today, the trend has turned the other way. About 80 percent of today's youth do not smoke cigarettes. Instead, drinking and smoking pot are on the rise. I hope the number of pot smokers has about peaked, but dealers can make so much money in dope, and users are younger and younger, so the numbers continue to rise.

Many people who have smoked for twenty years are now dying of cancer and heart and lung diseases. It hardly seems worth it now.

Look at the trends. Even though much of the scientific evidence isn't in, we do know people pay the price for their involvement in drugs for years to come. Say no, if you have the courage.

If you need reinforcement on how to creatively say no to drugs, you might want to go back to the chapter on raising your self-esteem and then the chapter on how to avoid peer pressure. We'll also talk about it at the end of this book.

Many experts say peer pressure is the number-one reason teens take drugs. I agree, but remember: The number-one reason for falling victim to negative peer pressure is low self-esteem. Raise your self-esteem, and you raise your chances to live a drug-free, normal life.

Check Out Your Turf

1. What makes drug use a huge national problem? What is the best answer to the problem in your life? How can you deal with it?

2. What is illicit drug use? Name the three ways drugs may be used illicitly.

3. What are psychoactive drugs? Name all seven kinds. Which are the most commonly used? Why?

4. Bill told a friend's story in this chapter. Do you think his story was unusual? Why or why not?

5. Is it hard to say no to drugs in your life now? How much harder is it to say no after a person has started using them? has used them for years? Is saying no now worth it?

11

HOW ABOUT ALCOHOL?

If you remember our definition from chapter eight, you won't have any trouble understanding why I say alcohol is a drug. If we call drugs addictive agents, booze certainly fits that bill. Many people say, "I'm not going to mess with drugs. I just drink." And the common weekend theme at many schools simply says, "Let's get some booze and cruise." It sounds cute, but that slogan leaves out one terrifying fact: Booze is the number-one killer of teens. Yes, it kills more teenagers than any other drug.

Facing the Facts

It's time to look at the facts about alcohol. Here are just a few:

Fact: The amount of alcohol in 12 ounces of beer = 1.5 ounces of 80 proof liquor = 5 ounces of wine.
Fact: Alcohol is a mind-altering drug. It works as a sedative.

Fact: A person can develop a strong psychological dependency on alcohol.

Fact: Alcohol is a serious problem. One out of every ten Americans who drink are problem drinkers.

Fact: There are over 8.5 million problem drinkers or alcoholics.

Fact: Recent research shows that women who drink during pregnancy run a greater risk of having smaller or deformed babies.

Fact: Alcohol abuse is the number-one drug problem among American teens and children.

Let's answer a few more questions—some on drinking this time.

Q: How many young people drink alcohol?

A: There are 3 million teenage alcoholics in America today. Most of them are also multiple drug users. (They smoke pot or do other drugs as well as drinking.)

Q: Why do people feel less inhibited when they drink?

A: Because the alcohol is absorbed through the digestive system into the bloodstream and reaches the brain quickly. It slows down the part of the brain that controls thinking and emotions. For this reason driving becomes greatly impaired while one is drinking.

Q: What determines how drunk a person will get?

A: Body weight, the amount of food in the person's system, and his tolerance level.

Q: Will coffee or cold showers or walking around make a drunk sober?

A: No. Coffee will give you a wide-awake drunk; showers give you a wet drunk; and walking gives you a tired drunk. Time alone sobers a drunk. A person who weighs 150 pounds will need about two hours to rid himself of the alcohol in one beer. A smaller person takes longer.

Do you know that if you have alcoholics in your family, you stand a much greater chance to become an alcoholic than if you don't? Don't start if you don't drink, and stop if you have started. I did. One day my brother Dale asked me if I believe it's right to put drugs into my system. I said, "No." He said, "Why don't you throw away all the booze behind your booze bar in your basement?" I didn't have any answer. So together we dumped every drop down the toilet. That was almost eight years ago. It was one of the best decisions of my life. I'm glad I made a strong commitment like that, because since then I've never gone back to drinking.

Students ask me quite often, "Should you drink?" I say, "Yes—water. If you don't, you'll die." But, *don't* drink booze. Booze kills and destroys. It kills brain cells and ambition. It destroys families, unborn babies, homes, jobs, promotions, enthusiasm, desires, relationships, hopes, dreams, friendships, marriages, fathers, and mothers. If you think the little bit of fun and pleasure you get seems worth it, look at all the negatives that go along with booze.

It's the same as all the possible problems and hurts and responsibilities that go along with the few minutes of pleasure of having sex with someone before you're married.

The prisons say, "If you can't do the time, don't do the crime." Others say, "If you can't stand the heat, stay out of the kitchen." It's the same with drugs and alcohol. "If you don't want to get burned, don't light up." "If you don't want to get hooked, don't get started."

You'll Hear About It Everywhere

Sure alcohol looks good. The media tell us all about it so often and in such rosy terms, it'd be hard not to feel some sense of attraction. It's difficult to get away from the message sent to us by movie stars and sports heroes that drinking is wonderful. But notice that the sports stars are always *ex* stars. While they were at the height of their careers, drinking such stuff would have been harmful to their performance. The smart ones never touched alcohol.

During the last summer Olympics I heard an ad for "the official Olympic beer." Talk about hypocrisy! Athletes caught drinking would have been kicked off their Olympic teams. Yet the money from such businesses helped build the running tracks, gymnasium, and swimming pools for those dedicated to avoiding such bad habits.

The stars who advertise drinking do not have to live with the results of it in their lives. If *you* drink, *you'll* have to pay.

Before you decide to start this habit, think about some more facts, about drinking today.

Alcohol is the number-one most used drug among teenagers (and their parents). The thing that scares me the most is the amount of alcohol kids drink. It seems that to prove yourself at a party, one beer isn't enough anymore. A six pack must be consumed, and the faster the better. Three out of every four junior and senior high school students drink, and one out of every five are problem drinkers.

Consider theses statistics:

> *Question:* What is the number-one killer of men and women in their teens and twenties?
> *Answer:* Drunk driving.
> *Question:* What crime is responsible for the deaths of 23,500 children and adults annually?
> *Answer:* Alcohol-related auto crashes.
> *Question:* What kills one American every 20 minutes?
> *Answer:* Alcohol-related auto crashes.
> *Question:* What seriously injures or cripples over 650,000 Americans every year?
> *Answer:* Drunk driving crashes.

I've just read a story from the magazine called *Group* (a youth-ministry magazine) about a fifteen-year-old Colorado high school student at a beer party. He paid a dollar to get into the party. While there, he drank nine cans of beer, a quart of bourbon, and a half bottle of whiskey. He left the party alone to walk home and was later found face up, dead, from acute alcohol poisoning. The other students said the party kind of got out of hand.

Here are my questions after such a senseless tragedy as this:

1. Why don't more people who promote these parties, along with the underage teens who are illegally drinking, get caught or punished?

2. Why don't more teens have the courage to do something about putting a stop to the number-one killer among them?

3. Why don't young people realize that booze kills? It kills brain cells and often kills innocent drivers on the highways after the fun party. At the funeral the students were asked, "What lesson did you learn from the death of your friend?" One replied, "I know he would want us to go on having a good time. He wouldn't want us to stop what we're doing."

People who drink and drive never think about others. They think of only one thing: me having fun *now!* They don't consider the mothers who are killed, leaving little babies forever without a mom, or entire families who are wiped out at one intersection. What about the hours and weeks of tears and mourning over lost fathers and friends, all because someone, young or old, had to drink and drive.

Hope for the Hopeless

His name is Gary, and his story has helped people of all ages and sizes to realize that no matter how bad your situation is, there is still hope.

He and his lovely wife had a child and what seemed to be the perfect family and future, but alcohol and stress crept in. Add to that all the frustrations in a fast-paced world, and before you know it, you've got a divorce.

Let's talk to Gary:

Bill: Gary, what was it like after your divorce? How did you deal with it?

Gary: It was terrible. I felt alone and frustrated. I needed a crutch to hold me up, so I drank more than I ever did before, and I turned to drugs.

Bill: What kind of drugs did you take?

Gary: Anything I could get my hands on. Any kind of pills would do.

Bill: But didn't you care what was inside them?

Gary: Are you kidding? As long as I got a buzz and got away from my problems, that was all that mattered.

Bill: Did they actually help you handle your problems?

Gary: No. They made them even worse, because now I *really* felt alone, and I had no means to get a job, and I was all strung out.

Bill: But you wear three-piece suits today, and you played college basketball. I can't imagine you on drugs.

Gary: I've got God to thank for that. He gave me the strength when I asked for it, and without His help I never would have made it. He sent people into my life at the time when I felt I had hit rock bottom.

Bill: How bad did things get?

Gary: I became a total doper. I barely had any money to live on, and most of that went for booze and drugs. I lived in an old garage with a dog. It was damp and cold, and I really felt like a prodigal son. I had lost my family, my future, and my dignity and self-respect.

Bill: What made you turn around?

Gary: I was out walking one Sunday morning when a van full of long-haired hippies pulled over and asked if I wanted to go to church with them. We went together, and afterward they prayed with me and asked how they could help. I told them about living in that old garage, and they insisted that I come and live with them.

Bill: Where did they live? Weren't you afraid to go with them?

Gary: They lived in a large house called House of Hope. They had a Christian ministry there. Some Christian businessmen bought the house, and the hippies used it to help people find God in a personal way. I had been a Christian since I was a boy, but I sure wasn't living it. I got back into God's Word and off drugs and booze.

Bill: Did you ever think there was a chance to get your ex-wife and child back?

Gary: Not really. I mean, I know that all things are possible with God, but I didn't love or even like my wife anymore. She couldn't stand me after all I had done to her. I didn't even like the thought of getting back together, but one thing kept ringing in my mind and heart.

Bill: What was that?

Gary: That God wanted us back together. The hippies prayed about it with me, and they said if God could change them from gutter drug abusers and give them an exciting purpose in life, then He could bring my family back together. They reminded me that God created the world and all that's in it in less than a week. He could surely do this, they told me. They said that God was the Creator of love, people, and the hearts where that love lives, and He could surely bring my love back alive for my wife. So after months of soul searching, I contacted my wife and told her about living in the house and going out with the hippies and reaching others for God. I also told her I felt it was God's purpose for us to get our family back together. She felt the same. Still we felt no love or attraction between us, but we decided to take the first step, and God would do the rest.

Bill: What happened?

Gary: We've got one of the happiest and strongest marriages anywhere in the world. She moved from Illinois out to California, where the house was, and the two of us ran the House of Hope for a year. We saw how God reaches the loneliest and the most impossible cases on earth. We've seen Him weld our family back together and bless us with three more beautiful children. Our priorities are simple. God and His will in our lives first. Our family second. Then my counseling and speaking career. I now counsel with couples who are having marital problems. I believe God molded me for this job. He pulled us through the impossible, and it gives hope to other people.

Bill: What advice would you give young people about drugs?

Gary: They are a cop-out! I used them to escape reality. I met a lot of druggies and alcoholics during the three years of my divorce. They hardly ever end up completely cured like me. Most of them end up dead, in jail, or in a mental institution. Drugs are a short-term escape with long-term effects. Drugs mean possibly living in an old, wet, dirty garage with an old, mangey dog. Drugs mean crying yourself to sleep at night. Do you know how much pride you lose when you are six foot four and you can't even look at yourself in the mirror? It hurts I tell you. It really hurts. I would beg young people to learn to say no to drugs. Don't even start. I've seen it over and over. They just try one joint or one upper or downer and then the next and on and on and on. If you are drinking and using it for a way out of your problems or reality—QUIT! Go to AA. I've begged kids before, and I'll beg them now. You've got too much to live for. Don't ruin your life.

Bill: Gary, I really appreciate your sharing from your heart like that. What do you tell people who have problems that seem hopeless and situations that seem helpless?

Gary: I tell them that on their own strength it may be helpless and hopeless. That's what our Creator is for. He made us, and He made us to need Him. He wants us to call on Him and lean on Him and to have Him show us a way to cope with our problems. I see teens, through my counseling practice, who are so depressed that they feel suicide or running away are the only answers. I share my story, and it often gives them hope. God can hold any problem on His shoulder. He can lift you up above it. Young people are strong. In fact, they are a lot stronger than most people think. I've seen them pull back from depression, the wrong crowd, drugs, atheism, not believing in themselves, and almost any conceivable problem. I leave them with this five-step formula.

1. Seek God's will. Find out what God really wants you to do. In our hearts we almost always know. I knew He wanted my wife and me back together, but I didn't want to have her back, because she wasn't appealing to me anymore. Kids know they should stop having sex before marriage or doing drugs, and so on.

2. Talk to others who have overcome the same problem you are going through. Go to counseling, AA, talk to a counselor at school, share with older and wiser people who love you and will sit and listen. That's what the hippies were to me. They gave me encouragement, because they made it through some unbelievable situations, too.

3. Write a commitment statement to yourself. Commit to a plan of action, and have others help you. Be accountable to someone. For instance, when I lived in the House of Hope I had others who were committed to me, and I promised them I would never drink. I couldn't let them down, no matter how bad things got. This is like a specific goal. Tackle yours step by step.

4. Pray to God for help every step of the way. Include your family, telling them you need their help and support.

5. Stick to your commitment statement. This is like a contract between you and you. It can be between you and God. Picture in your mind being free from your problem. I used to picture a good, happy marriage again. Now, with God's help, I've got the impossible. You can have it, too. Go for it!

Where Do We Go From Here?

Gary's story really meant a lot to me when I first heard it. It gave me hope over some of my so-called impossible situations. Seeing Gary's full-time counseling practice become a reality and his speaking career flourish really makes me feel great, because he is one of my two best friends in the entire world. You see, I'm his speaking mentor. Together we work on the finest details of his speeches. I laugh with him over his successes, and I hurt with him during his failures. When Gary challenged you to commit to a plan of action, I can tell you that he practices what he preaches. I've challenged him to give eighty speeches in one year, and he is working hard to make it happen.

It Takes No Effort at All

That's right, it takes almost no effort at all to turn into a nothing—a nobody. It is the easiest thing in the world to be a bum—a person who never tries or never fails or never succeeds. It's like my friend Larry Moles said. He saw an old wino lying on the sidewalk, and when he asked him how he ended up that way, the old man replied, "It don't take much to be like me."

Don't let alcohol do that to you. Have the courage to fight back. Give it up—or even better, never start with it at all.

Check Out Your Turf

1. Why is alcohol considered a drug? Do you agree that it is? Why or why not?
2. What did you learn about alcohol in this chapter? Has it changed your thinking about drinking? Why or why not?
3. Why do you think drinking is often so well accepted by society? Does it make sense? What can you do to help those who are thinking about trying drinking? How can you stand up to peer pressure on your own?
4. What was Gary's five-step formula for overcoming a drinking problem? Do you think it could be used for other problems? Name some.

Suggested Reading List

If you want to do more study on drugs contact the following publishers and ask for information about these publications.

PUBLISHER	AUTHOR	TITLE
American Council for Drug Education 6193 Executive Blvd. Rockville, Maryland 20852	Richard Hawley	A School Answers Back Responding to student drug use
National Institute on Drug Abuse Div. of Prevention and Communication Prevention Branch 5600 Fishers Lane Rockville, Maryland 20857	Tom Adams and Hank Resnik	Teens in Action
Health Communications Inc. 2119-A Hollywood Blvd. Hollywood, Florida 33020		Parents, Peers and Pot
Committees of Correspondence, Inc. P.O. Box 232 Topsfield, MA 01983	Connie and Otto Moulton	Partial list of prodrug books with misleading information and information on their authors
	Dr. Susan L. Dalterio Susan Bromwell	Marijuana and the Unborn How I Got My Daughter To Stop Smoking Pot Drugs, Drinking, and Adolescents (Also ask for their New Member Package)
National Institute of Drug Abuse Office of Communications and Public Affairs 5600 Fishers Lane Rockville, Maryland 20857	Don Wilkerson	For Kids Only What you should know about marijuana
Fleming H. Revell Company 184 Central Avenue Old Tappan, New Jersey 07675		Marijuana
McGraw-Hill 1221 Avenue of the Americas New York, NY 10020	Peggy Mann	Marijuana Alert

WHERE DO I GO FROM HERE?

Maybe you think that with this book I'm trying to tell you you have to make changes in your life. I hope I am! I've aimed *Tough Turf* at helping you spiritually, emotionally, physically, financially, and socially. Lots of effort goes into that kind of change. If you want to follow through, you'll need to do some hard work, and it'll take a lot of commitment. But it'll be worth it—count on it! You *can* do it.

So What'll It Take?

You may have to make the word *no* a really active part of your vocabulary, if you haven't already. Now you know some of the bad things that can happen to you if you say yes too quickly. But you also know what a special person you are (you've already proved it by finishing this book—it makes you one of the 10 percent of Americans who have read a book this year!).

Maybe you're thinking that if you follow my advice you'll have to stay away from every party where there's a chance of booze or drugs showing up. That's up to you. However, you will probably stay away from every social gathering in your town, if you do. It's a tough decision. But if you know it's a "kegger" or that someone's bringing dope, think about staying away, if you don't want to take the chance of being arrested for breaking the law. By the way, parents who give alcohol to their kids and their kids' friends can be sued if anything happens to the kids.

Ask yourself this: When you go to parties and booze or drugs show up, what will you do? Will you have enough courage to say no and walk away? Or if you date a guy who thinks sex is okay before marriage, will you be able to say no? What if both of you have a few drinks, you lose your inhibitions, and you end up pregnant? If a girl gets pregnant because she doesn't have the nerve to say no (for whatever reason), very few guys stick around long enough to help, much less provide support through thick and thin.

If you lose your reputation, no one can bring it back for you. If you're a pregnant girl, you have to live alone with the results, because chances are the guy is gone long before you can ask if he really loves you. If you get a reputation for drinking, for pushing drugs, you'll have to live with that. Your teachers and parents, once they catch on to what's going on, might start treating you differently. And chances are you won't like the change at all.

For these and other situations, you'll need to practice saying the word no. But today that isn't just a matter of facing up to the person who offers you the drug (or alcohol) or who wants some sex. You face hidden pressures all around you—even though you might not be at all aware of them.

Have you seen the way the media sell harmful substances like tobacco and alcohol? They don't come out and tell you, "This is bad for you, but we want you to buy it anyway." They do it subliminally—subconsciously. They don't ask your permission to tell you about it. They don't twist your arm to take the first puff. You probably don't notice the effect it's having on you.

Years ago advertisers would flash a quick picture of a popcorn and Coke on the screen during a movie. At the break, sales soared. Everybody got thirsty and hungry, but they didn't know why. Such advertising is now illegal, but the folks who sell goods still use subliminal advertising techniques to sell their products—they just use different ones. How about the typical billboard ad? It shows one guy in the middle, with girls all around. He'll have lipstick all over his head. What's the company selling? Sex appeal, not cigarettes. It's just as though the cigarette walked on center stage, grabbed a microphone, and said to gullible young Americans, "If you smoke me, you'll be so glamorous that no one of the opposite sex can possibly resist you." That's crazy, because if you think about it, kissing someone who smokes is just like licking an ashtray.

When a teen comes up to me and says, "I'll have you know I smoke," I answer, "No, you don't. The cigarette smokes. You're just the sucker." Don't fall for such ploys that would take control of your life. Your life belongs to you, not the cigarette manufacturer. So take control of yours, or someone else will run your life for you.

Before you start on dope, remember that *you're* going to be the dope, whether you smoke it, eat it, or do it. One joint has the power to leave over four hundred deadly poisons in your system for up to thirty days. Regular THC users can expect it to build up and stay in their fat cells and do its damage for the next month. For six to ten hours after a high, THC slows the user's reflexes considerably, making driving dangerous. And those are just a few of the short-term effects.

We're seeing teenage mothers who smoked during pregnancy have babies with no skull—the brains are exposed! Some young people who have done drugs have gone numb all over, never to recover.

Right now you might be snickering to yourself, thinking, *He doesn't know what he's talking about. These are just scare tactics.* I know what I'm talking about. For three years I smoked pot recreationally. I never thought anything would happen either. But today I'm convinced that the reason I can't have children of my own is that I damaged my reproductive organs during those three years of dope use. I have to live with that the rest of my life.

What you do today can influence the rest of your life—for good or bad! Today people are going blind from getting high twenty years ago. You think it's impossible? Here's what happened. Pushers cut the dope with anything that will make it go farther. They cut cocaine with baby powder. The cocaine breaks down in the system, but baby powder doesn't. It takes fifteen years for the powder to flow through the system and end up in the eye. People are literally going blind, twenty years later.

How To Say No

If someone offers you any drug, legal or illegal, here are twenty ways of saying no.

1. "No!"
2. "No thank you."
3. "I'm not a dope."
4. "I never do the stuff."
5. "I don't believe in it."
6. "Thanks, but no thanks."
7. "I'm not into destroying my brain cells."
8. "I'm not going to pickle my heart, barbecue my lungs, burn my brains, fry my chromosomes, frazzle my cells or coat all my fatty tissues with THC."
9. "I'm into a great future, not a wrecked here and now."
10. "My body is the only vehicle I get in this life, and I'm not going to put junk into it."
11. "My body is a temple of the Lord, and there's no room for God *and* dope inside."
12. "Absolutely not."
13. "Not today."

14. "No, no, never, never, uh-uh."
15. "Not me, no, sir."
16. "What—dope? Are you crazy?"
17. "Would you chew on dynamite just because someone said it would give you a buzz?"
18. "I'm not stupid. Are you?"
19. "I may be dumb, but I'm not stupid. The answer is absolutely, positively *no*."
20. "My buddy did it, and he's dead. The answer is *no*, and don't ask again."

You can use some of the same methods to say no to other bad things in your life. Even if you've been involved in something that's destroying your life, you can start saying no now. Don't wait for twenty years. Saying that small, hard word won't be easier then—it'll be more difficult, and your life will be more of a mess.

God can help put back together anything you've pulled apart. In my life, the happiest, most exciting accomplishments have been in my family and spiritual growth. It wasn't always like that. After Holly and I had been married just three years, we came very close to getting a divorce. I was unfaithful, and my actions led to the near collapse of our marriage. Because I put God on the throne of my life and in our lives, I can excitedly say that I'm not just married to my wife, but I'm married to my best friend. After ten years, I am still "in love" with Holly. Our marriage doesn't just exist, instead we have an exciting adventure every day. With our only child, little Emily, whom the Lord gave us through adoption, our cup is surely full.

I'd like to challenge you the way I challenge the students I talk to. I ask them to stand to signify they're stopping any of the bad habits I've mentioned: tobacco, dope, booze, and sex before marriage. It's exciting to see kids who don't fear publicly making a stand. I can't ask you to stand in front of a crowd, but your actions can speak louder than any public one-time motion like that. If people see the change in your life, they'll *know* something has happened. Let them see that in yours.

How to Say Yes

Saying no to all the bad influences in your life doesn't mean just chucking everything out. You're going to have to put good things in the place of the negative influences. Reread Part I to get some ideas for new habits and actions you want in your life. Start working on a positive plan—one that will help you be the best you can be.

You *are* special. Others have done it, and so can you. I have faith in you—have some in yourself.

It Takes Courage

I've got one final story for you. I always tell this last, because it's touched me personally in so many ways. It's helped me to come up with the courage it takes to make it in this world today. I hope it touches you the way it has the over 1 million young people who have already heard it.

Her name is Nikki. In the seventh grade she came down with leukemia. At an age where peer pressure is so vital, she heard the worst news a person could ever hear: "You may die soon." Her family is strong and close, and they pulled together in a way that has inspired an entire community.

Because of her treatments and therapy, Nikki lost all of her beautiful, light brown hair. It didn't grow back, and everyone began to worry. The kids at her school called her names and snickered. I guess you weren't there to stop it or to tell them that "the wrong kind of laughter" won't be tolerated in this school.

She has said, "It's not so bad that I've lost my hair—I can deal with that. It's not even so bad I'm losing my life—I know that by believing in God as my Savior I'll go to heaven, so I can deal with that. What really hurts is losing my friends. They don't like to eat at my table anymore in the cafeteria. Do you know what it's like to eat all alone and have the other kids look at and whisper about you? It really hurts. It also hurts when I'm avoided in the hallways and classrooms. Don't they know that when I am hurting I just need someone to hurt with me and to listen to me. I need someone to simply be there. That's when I needed their friendship most of all."

That summer her hair didn't grow back, so she wore a wig to school, but you know kids. They couldn't resist pulling on it. Can you imagine how embarrassing it would be to have your wig pulled off in front of other students? *In the eighth grade!* It happened several times the first week or so of school, and it almost killed her, but this girl was a hero! She had courage—the kind you only hear about once in a great while. She's my hero, not Michael Jackson or Bruce Springsteen. Here's why. She got strong. She and her family really put God first. Her dad passed up several job promotions, because he wanted her to be with her classmates and not have to move. Her mom was also such an encouragement and filled with more love and commitment than many people have in a lifetime. Even her younger brother didn't mind if she got all the attention. He prayed for her and wasn't afraid to hug her in public. They put God first, then their family right behind. It was their foundation on which to stand firm, no matter how tough things got.

The next week, on the way to school, she did something that has inspired thousands and thousands to have the courage to do the things they have to do.

Her parents took her to school each day, and as unpopular as it seems, they hugged and kissed every morning before she got out of the car and went into school. This morning she said to her parents, "Guess what I'm going to do today?" "What, honey?" they asked, sensing the seriousness in her tone of voice. She replied with tear-filled eyes, "Today I'm going to find out who my real friends are. I prayed all night about it, and I know God has given me you as my family and His love, so I can make it through today. I've got to know who my real friends are. I've got to know who likes me for me and not for what I look like or if I've got leukemia or not—but for me." With that, she pulled the wig off her head and set it on the seat beside her, and as she got out of the car she said, "Pray for me." They said, "We are, honey. You can do it. We're with you all the way." She got out, looked back for a brief moment, then started walking across that junior high playground. She walked right through the middle of 600 students, and a miracle happened that day. No one, not the bullies or the loudmouths, made fun of her or her hairless head. They just stood and watched her walk into school and admired her courage.

She changed that entire school and community. Her courage has helped many many young people like you who need a little oomph to make it through life's tough times.

Guess what? They didn't laugh at her, and they won't laugh at you, if you have the courage to stand for something greater than your own fears and worries. Put God first, the way Nikki and her family have. Believe in your family and yourself. Re-open those love channels at home. Talk and make the first step toward making your homelife strong. Do what is right. As you begin to walk in the right paths you will see changes in your life. Nikki's life looked pretty grim in seventh grade, but today she is doing fine. Her disease went into remission, and she just graduated from high school. During the summer she travels all over the world with traveling theater groups. She uses her life to inspire people. You can do the same.

You don't have to go it alone. God won't give up on you, but He will be right there with you. He never told you you have to win—but He does want you to try. Even though you may never make the team or be a straight-A student, I can promise you a relationship with God will make your life better.

You can do it. Go for it!

If you'd like to share something with me, I'd like to hear from you, pray for you, or know what you think of *Tough Turf*. Drop me a line at:

Bill Sanders
P.O. Box 711
Portage, MI 49081

I also may be contacted there to arrange speaking engagements at schools, conventions for young people or adults, or at other meetings.
